Tribal Class Destroyers

ROYAL NAVY AND COMMONWEALTH

Peter Hodges

ALMARK PUBLISHING CO. LTD., LONDON

First published — November 1971

ISBN 0 85524 046 6 (hard cover edition)
ISBN 0 85524 047 4 (paper covered edition)

By the same Author:
Battle Class Destroyers
British Military Markings, 1939-1945

Printed in Great Britain by
Martins Press Ltd., London EC1
for the publishers, Almark Publishing Co. Ltd.,
270 Burlington Road, New Malden,
Surrey KT3 4NL, England.

Introduction

IN the successive decades of destroyer construction dating from 1930, three peaks were reached. Standing upon the highest—the 'Darings'—and looking through time over the terrain of classes, the 'Battles' lie close : and perhaps it is perspective alone that makes them seem slightly lower.

Beyond them, and fading as memory fades, is the valley of the Emergency Classes, whose deepest point marks the 'O' class. Here, there starts a sharp incline, rising to a great peak that to some is still sharp and clear.

This book is about that peak—the 'Tribal' class. To those who remember them, I hope it will serve as a means of preserving the clarity of that distant crest. For those who never knew them, perhaps it will convey something of their pre-eminence.

My thanks are due to the following for their permission to reproduce the photographs herein :

The Imperial War Museum
The Public Archives of Canada
The Royal Australian Navy
P. A. Vicary, of Cromer, Norfolk
Ministry of Defence
Anthony Pavia, of Birkirkara, Malta
Messrs Ron Forrest and Associates (late Wright and Logan) of Southsea
Messrs Vickers (Shipbuilders) Limited

I am especially grateful to Mrs Beryl Fraser, of Toronto, Canada, for her kind help.

This volume follows the pattern of my previous book about the 'Battles', and illustrates all 'Tribals' built at various stages of their service. The book is essentially devoted to the ships themselves and their weapons system—the guns—and does not presume to tell the story of their eventful operational careers. Official histories and many other publications have already done just that, and many exploits involving 'Tribals'—notably the *Altmark* incident and the Malta Convoys—are well recorded elsewhere.

CONTENTS

ABOVE: In March 1949, HMCS Athabaskan *sticks her bow into the green Atlantic as she comes alongside the carrier* Magnificent. *At that time the Mk 6 director on the bridge still had a rangefinder, but this was later removed. This ship was the last 'Tribal' actually in active commission. (Public Archives of Canada).*

A Channel sweep in 1944, with Haida *in company with* Huron *and a 'Modified Dido' class cruiser—probably* Diadem—*in the background. In April 1944* Haida *avenged the first* Athabaskan *by driving her sister ship's killer ashore. She was in the Cherbourg action in June and in the same month joined* Eskimo *in the destruction of U-971 (Public Archives of Canada).*

FRONT COVER: HMS Nubian *in 1944 while serving with the Eastern Fleet. Pictured when closing HMS* Renown *to refuel, she exhibits all the wartime changes incorporated in surviving 'Tribals', notably the lattice mast and radar arrays. Note the windscoops in the forward scuttles (P. A. Vicary).*

Chapter 1: Development

DESPITE the not inconsiderable success of the standard form of British pre-war destroyer as an 'export model' among the minor navies of the world, by the mid-1930s it was becoming increasingly clear that a much more powerful design was required for the Royal Navy if Britain was to maintain parity with the destroyers of about 2,000 tons emerging from the shipyards of the other major powers.

From 1929 onwards, a new flotilla of eight vessels plus an enlarged 'Leader' was launched on a more-or-less annual basis, culminating in the 'I' class which entered the water between late 1936 and early 1937. (The phrase 'more-or-less' is used deliberately because the precise building programme of these groups is not our concern.) These ships were regarded—somewhat fondly—as 'classical British destroyers' but unfortunately they had inherent weaknesses which were to cost them dear in the Second World War.

For while, in 1929, their capabilities in terms of armament, speed and range were ahead of contemporary ships built abroad, these advantages were gradually eroded away as the 1930s progressed, largely because the design itself was not altered in any radical way.

Among the higher echelons of the British Naval Staff, opinions on destroyer armament and general concept were divided. Some saw only too clearly how serious were the inherent shortcomings, but were hamstrung by a parsimonious Exchequer and the inevitable need to compromise. In consequence, little real attention was paid towards the fire control and anti-aircraft capabilities of the type as a whole.

Until the 'C' and 'D' classes—launched in 1931–32—no British destroyers had a proper fire control predictor for surface fire, all the earlier ships relying on a simple Pedestal Director Sight mounted on the bridge, in association with a separate range-finder, and a rudimentary 'Range Clock'. It is true that the 'As' and 'Bs' were eventually given the Admiralty Fire Control Clock Mk II as a retrospective fitting, but the later 'Destroyer DCT', coupled to the Admiralty Fire Control Clock Mk I, was not a standard fitting until the half flotilla of 'C' class (as well as RCN *Saguenay* and *Skeena*) came into service.

The maximum elevation of the main armament 4·7-inch guns was pushed up from 30° in the Mk XIV mounting to 40° in the Mk XVIII of the 'H' and 'I' classes (with an unsatisfactory interim arrangement of removable deck plates to enable the 30° Mk XVII of the 'E', 'F' and 'G' classes to reach 40°). But if the need for a true dual-purpose gun design was realised before the war, for one reason or another, it was not followed up. Thus, with the 'I' class, Britain had produced a destroyer whose anti-aircraft defence capabilities were really little better than those of the prototypes *Amazon* and *Ambuscade*, launched a decade earlier.

Neither the 'Is' nor any of their predecessors had an AA predictor, and were

The twin 4·7-inch era began with the installation of the prototype in 'B' position in HMS Hereward, *here passing the Gosport shore line as she leaves Portsmouth for trials on December 21, 1936.* Hereward *was typical of the 'between-wars' destroyer classes, but had the modified bridge front containing the steering position, which was raised to overlook the new mounting's gunshield. A large number of these mountings was produced—64 for the RN 'Tribals', 72 for the 'J', 'K' and 'N' classes, plus a further 20-odd for the Commonwealth ships, although the latter may have received some 'X' mounting 'discards' (Wright & Logan).*

weakly armed in the close-range sense. The early hand-worked single 2-pdr (which at least had some hitting power) had been replaced by the quad 0·5-inch Vickers machine-gun mounting—a weapon with neither the range nor the destructive power to stop a modern aircraft. Thus, while these destroyers made a brave sight as they sped along in line ahead at 35 knots, they were, in fact, hopelessly under-gunned.

The policy of designing destroyers to act as fast mine-sweepers, in the main reduced their anti-submarine equipment to two depth-charge throwers and one short overstern rail, but fortunately this was not irredeemable, because the removal of the 'Two Speed Destroyer's Sweep' gear—and its replacement by a doubled-up depth-charge armament—was comparatively simple. In the same way, the conventionally mounted torpedo tubes could be rapidly removed in favour of other weapons.

All these early classes suffered greviously in the war, and as it progressed, the survivors were almost all relegated to an escort rôle. With no adequate long-range AA defence they had become unsuitable for Fleet work and in consequence even those with a surface DCT and Fire Control Clock had them removed to create space for the surface warning radar 'lantern' and increased A/S weapons.

Such then were the classes leading up to the 'Tribals'; and the critic might be forgiven were he to conclude that the British Naval Staff of the day were somewhat short-sighted. Be that as it may, the Admiralty was to produce a handsome ship when the design of the new class was finalized.

Initially, there was much discussion on the armament layout which at one time envisaged no less than 10 4·7-inch guns in five twin mountings. Finally, when all considerations of ultimate maximum speed and top-weight were taken into account, it was decided to fit four twin 4·7's sited in the conventional 'A', 'B', 'X' and 'Y' positions (or 1, 2, 3 and 4 to use pre-war parlance); one quadruple 2-pdr pompom on the forward end of the long after superstructure; 'sided' multiple 0·5-inch Vickers machine-guns between the funnels; and one quadruple torpedo tube mounting abaft the second funnel.

Compared with the earlier classes, the 'Tribals' were little short of revolutionary, and must have created much the same impact on the Fleet as had

6

This is the 4·7-inch Mk XIV mounting, fitted in the 'A' and 'B' class destroyers. Note the breech-worker's platform on the right and the loading tray on the left, carried on one of a pair of support tubes which terminated in the balance weight. When, in later single mountings, the breech-end was shifted towards the trunnions to increase the maximum elevation, a heavier balance weight was required. This was supported by a framework over the breech and loading tray—a scheme adopted in the twin 4·7-inch. Of particular interest are the old-style 'ready-use' shell stowages surrounding the gundeck and the deck overlay of corticene, secured by polished brass strips (P. A. Vicary).

Dreadnought years previously. Not only had the Admiralty doubled the number of guns, but they had halved the torpedo armament.

The latter move was most interesting in the light of subsequent events; for although later classes reverted to the 8 or 10 torpedo tube arrangement, a large number of destroyers had one set removed during the war (to increase the gun armament!), so the 'Tribals' were not at that time any the worse off in this respect.

Continuing their long established, and very sensible policy of spreading the contracts around the shipbuilding centres of Great Britain, the Admiralty awarded the first two to Vickers' Tyneside yard, two to Fairfield, two to Thornycroft and the seventh to Alexander Stephen. This initial order was quickly followed by a repeat for nine more, the extra ship squaring up the total to 16. Vickers again got two, the others being shared equally between Denny, Scotts and Swan Hunter, with Stephen taking the odd one. Most shipyards built their own engines, but Vickers sub-contracted the machinery either to their own yard at Barrow-in-Furness or to Parsons, while Swan Hunter employed Wallsend Shipyard further down the Tyne.

The first seven officially came from the 1935 estimates, and the remainder from those of the next year but, in fact, the only ship not to be laid down between June and November 1936 was *Bedouin*, whose keel was laid in January 1937. Building proceeded apace, so that in a year all 16 had been launched.

A change in policy deleted an enlarged ninth ship to act as Leader for each group of eight; instead four ships were fitted out with increased accommodation for Leader's duties, but were externally indistinguishable from their sisters—except, of course, for their black fore-funnel band and the absence of pendant numbers on the ship's side and stern.

It is worth mentioning here, that Captain (D) (to which title the flotilla number was added) was in command of his own ship and at the same time assumed operational and administrative control of his flotilla. He would,

Alphabetically first, and Leader of the initial group, HMS Afridi was built by Vickers Armstrong on the Tyne, but was engined by Vickers, Barrow-in-Furness. Here, early in 1938, she is on CSTs (Contractor's Sea Trials), wearing the Red Ensign aft and Vickers' House Flag at the main gaff (IWM).

quite literally, 'lead' them into action, making a succession of flag signals like 'Attack with torpedoes', 'Follow me', and so on. In the days of visual signalling, this kept the signalmen of all ships in company very busy indeed, for it was no joke hoisting a flag group to the yardarm in a wind speed across the deck in excess of 30 knots.

Each of the specialist officers in the Leader also assumed flotilla duties, so that the Gunnery Officer became the *Flotilla* Gunnery Officer, the Torpedo Officer the *Flotilla* Torpedo Officer, etc. In some branches, two specialist

Afridi, commissioned in May 1938, made a splendid sight as she left Portsmouth soon afterwards. The 'Tribal' ships' companies can hardly be blamed for considering themselves the élite of the destroyer men. This ship was the second of her class to be lost, succumbing to German bombs off Namsos, but her captain, Captain Phillip Vian, RN, survived to command Cossack—and ultimately reached the rank of Admiral of the Fleet (Wright & Logan).

officers were borne in the Leader herself, and this was particularly so in the engine room department. There was almost always a Commander (E) as Flotilla Engineer Officer, supported for 'Ship duties' by a Warrant Engineer. The latter functioned as the Ship's Engineer, leaving his Commander free to worry about the engineering problems of the whole flotilla, and particularly their individual refits.

Captain (D) also had specialist staff officers of branches other than those normally carried in a destroyer, but all could not be found accommodation in the Leader, and some were spread among the flotilla.

Taking *Afridi* as a typical flotilla Leader, the set-up in 1938 was:

Captain	In command and as Captain (D)
	1st (Tribal) Destroyer Flotilla
1st Lieutenant	Second-in-command
	(of ship only)
Gunnery Officer	
Torpedo Officer	
Navigation Officer	And for flotilla duties
Engineer Commander	
Supply Officer	
Surgeon Lieutenant	
Paymaster Lieutenant	Captain's Secretary
Warrant Engineer	Ship duties
Commissioned Ordnance Officer ⎫	Accommodated in *Zulu*
Warrant Schoolmaster ⎰	(for flotilla duties)
Torpedo Gunner ⎱	Accommodated in *Cossack*
Warrant Telegraphist ⎰	(for flotilla duties)

If the Leader was lost in action, command reverted to the 'Half Leader' (who might also be a full Captain RN) and then in succession through the other Commanding Officers in order of seniority.

In addition to the above, there would probably be two or three junior

The old 'genouin (genuine) Bedouin' in April 1939. One can almost imagine that the war clouds are gathering over her as she enters Portsmouth harbour, less than a month after commissioning. She wears a dark funnel band on the after funnel, which was changed in May 1939 to white. Notice the 'Right of Way' hoist flying from the yardarm. The paint finish is clean and immaculate and on the original print there is clear evidence of careful 'touching up' on the ship's side (Wright & Logan).

The splendid Cossack *enjoys ideal conditions for her CSTs in the Tyne area in 1938. She was a Portsmouth-manned ship and first commissioned in June 1938 under the command of Captain D. de Pass, RN. She wears a 'half-leader' band on her fore funnel in preparation for her duties as Divisional Leader of the 1st (Tribal) Destroyer Flotilla, Mediterranean—NOT to be confused with the 1st DF proper. This special 'Tribal' flotilla eventually became the 4th DF and did not employ a flotilla band. The white and blue swallow-tailed flag is the somewhat laconic International Code signal meaning 'Undergoing speed trials' (IWM).*

officers or midshipmen borne temporarily for training. It was usual also, for the Leader to carry 'key' senior ratings. For example, 'D' would have a Chief Yeoman of Signals on his bridge, whereas the other ships might only be entitled to a Petty Officer Yeoman. On the other hand, because *Afridi* herself had two Engineer Officers on her Ship's Book, the Senior Chief Engine Room Artificer would be carried, perhaps in the 'Half Leader'.

An early intention seems to have been to use the 'Tribals' individually, to stiffen the fire power and general resources of the existing flotillas of lighter destroyers; but when the first ships commissioned in 1938, they were formed up into the 1st (Tribal) Destroyer Flotilla, Mediterranean. This comprised the seven vessels of the original order plus *Sikh*, the first of the nine 'repeats' to be accepted.

Three ships of the remaining eight—*Ashanti, Eskimo* and *Somali*—commissioned in December 1938 and since *Somali* was intended as a Leader anyway, she was earmarked to lead the 2nd (Tribal) Destroyer Flotilla.

Her first Commanding Officer, Captain R. S. G. Nicholson, D.S.C., RN, was appointed 'in command, and as Captain (D) 2nd (Tribal) Destroyer Flotila (designate)', but there was a further general reorganization of destroyer flotillas, and this designation was not proceeded with.

The remaining seven ships all commissioned in the early part of 1939 to run in the Home Fleet and, when war broke out, those in the Mediterranean (which at that time was not the busy war zone it was later to become) were pulled out. So, in early 1940, when the bulk of the British destroyer strength was in home waters, one group of 'Tribals' formed the 4th Flotilla and the second became the 6th Flotilla.

Thereafter they were used collectively in decreasing numbers as their sisters were lost, until the wheel turned full circle, and 'Tribals' were found mixed

Eskimo was Chatham manned and commissioned in December 1938 under the command of Commander St. J. A. Micklethwaite, RN. She was one of the four fortunate 'Tribals' to go right through the war—but hardly unscathed, for her bow was blown off by a torpedo in the second battle of Narvik. Notice the red/white/blue recognition bands worn by British warships during the Spanish Civil War (Wright & Logan).

among other destroyer types—a policy mooted at their inception. In any case, as the war in Europe progressed, there were never enough fleet destroyers to meet the demand, and they were mostly forced to operate in groups of between three and five ships. Thus, one found *Cossack, Sikh, Zulu* and the Polish *Piorun* in the *Bismark* action; *Sikh, Maori, Legion* and the Dutch *Isaac Sweers* engaging Italian cruisers; and *Sikh, Lively, Hero* and *Havock* in the second battle of Sirte.

When Italy sued for peace, the intensity of the naval war in the Mediterranean diminished, but by this time only four of the original 16 ships were afloat. These were *Ashanti, Eskimo, Nubian* and *Tartar*, who were then refitted and modernized. Three joined forces with the early Canadian 'Tribals' on Channel sweeps immediately prior to the Normandy landings, culminating in the destroyer action off Cherbourg in June 1944, while *Nubian* went out to the East Indies to join the Eastern Fleet.

In 1945 the four British ships re-formed in the East Indies as the 10th Flotilla, lead by *Tartar* (which fortunately had been fitted from building as a Leader), under the command of Captain (D10) B. Jones, D.S.O. and Bar, D.S.C., RN, but their working lives were almost over and by 1949 the last had gone for scrap.

Cossack in the Mediterranean in 1938 when her acceptance trials were over. The ship's company are at 'Stations for leaving harbour', dressed in their full white Tropical No. 6 dress. This was cynically referred to as the 'ice-cream suit' and looked extremely smart but became soiled very quickly. (A. & J. Pavia).

Looking aft from the fo'c'sle at 'A' and 'B' mountings. The cartridge ready-use locker on the starboard side has two vacant tubes—probably because their charges have been placed in readiness on the loading trays. The young seaman wearing the headset is 'A' gun communication number, but it is unlikely that the full gun's crew is closed up, because the sighting ports are closed. The majority of the personnel have 'blue' caps, but two ratings on 'B' gundeck have white tops, which at this time were only worn in the Tropics or in Home waters in the summer. Note the white topmast (IWM).

Chapter 2: Machinery and Armament

THE 'Tribals' were notable in incorporating a number of 'firsts' and 'lasts' in their layout. In so far as the hull was concerned, they were the last to employ the established transverse framing; and they also ended a long run of twin-funnelled destroyers. Indeed, only the post-war 'Weapons' and 'Darings' re-introduce this scheme, and then for special reasons beyond the scope of the present subject.

Internally, the arrangements conformed to contemporary practice. In broad terms, the crew's quarters were forward of the break of the fo'c'sle; the main machinery compartments were in the waist and the officers' cabins and wardroom aft.

There had been a good deal of juggling with the division of the Boiler Rooms/Engine Room/Gearing Compartment in earlier classes, but in the 'Tribals' there were five separate spaces. The three boilers were contained in separate boiler rooms, the uptakes of the forward and centre being trunked into the fore-funnel, and those of the after boiler to the narrower after funnel. Each boiler room had an Admiralty Three Drum Boiler working at 300lb p.s.i. and in the engine room—immediately abaft the third boiler room—there were two Parsons' single reduction turbines. They developed 44,000 Shaft Horse-power at 350 r.p.m. giving a nominal speed of 36 knots but, in service, it is unlikely that a sea-speed of 34 knots was exceeded, except on trials. Abaft the engine room, the turbine outputs were geared down in a gearing compartment to drive the two propellor shafts.

As well as turbo-generators for electric power, there were also two turbo-hydraulic units. Each consisted of a steam turbine driving a pair of radial hydraulic pumps, supplying power to the forward and after groups of 4·7-inch mountings. In the event of failure of one pump, two mountings of the same group could be linked to the other.

The total oil fuel capacity was slightly more than 500 tons and this gave a radius action of 5,700 miles at an economical speed of 15 knots. Above that speed the graph of oil consumption rose sharply on a steeping slope so that the range decreased to 3,000 miles at just over 20 knots, and progressively thereafter.

THE ORIGINAL ARMAMENT

The development trials on a new twin 4·7-inch mounting were carried out in HMS *Hereward*, which was temporarily equipped with the prototype, but subsequently exchanged it for her normal single Mk XVIII when the trials were complete.

This weapon became the 4·7-inch Twin Mk XIX and carried two QF Mk XII

A fine photograph looking down from the mast on to the bridge and the forward twin 4·7s. The working area of the bridge deck has wooden gratings which were less tiring to weary feet than steel decks. The area seems somewhat crowded with busy officers and the Captain (wearing the 'brass hat') looks mightily disinterested— perhaps wishing that his bridge was a little less full. He is probably Captain (D) because the Chief Petty Officer on the port side is a Chief Yeoman of Signals—(D)s right-hand man in action. The guns are trained on to 'look-out' bearings, and a 'cruising watch' is closed up on 'B' while army personnel look on. Two soldiers have moved forward to the 'eyes' of the ship to watch the stem as it slices through the water. Like their companions, they are prudently wearing life-jackets. Notice the ready-use shell stowages around the gundecks; the ropes within the blast shield over 'A' gun; the glass windscreen on the forebridge; the gyro compass binnacle; and the secondary magnetic compass binnacle flanked by voice pipes abaft it (IWM).

guns in a common cast steel cradle. It was the first twin and the first power mounting constructed specifically for destroyer main armament.

In single-gun mountings with horizontal sliding breech blocks, the loading tray was on the left, and the breech opened away from it, towards the right, controlled by the breech worker who stood on that side.

This was obviously impossible to arrange on the left gun of the twin mounting, so a new left-hand breech mechanism had to be designed. Further, of course, there was also a 'right' gun which became a sort of mirror image of its partner.

The breech blocks opened inwards towards each other, and although there was sufficient clearance for both to be open at the same time, they could only be removed for stripping in sequence. The blocks were fitted for percussion or electric firing, the latter being the normal method in Director Control.

In local—or 'Quarters'—firing both guns could be fired together, or independently, by a gunlayer's foot pedal; and there was separate provision for independent percussion firing by either breech worker.

The turbo-hydraulic pumps referred to earlier, delivered oil at 1,000 p.s.i.

Loading on the 4·7-inch Mk XIX mounting. The gun cradle carrying the two guns is
extended to the rear above the breeches by a heavy framework, terminating in the
balance weights. Slung beneath them, but not visible in this photo, were two cylinders
filled with air at high pressure, called 'recuperators'. A ram slid through a gland in the
forward part of the cylinder and its other extremity was connected to a lug, machined
on to the breech ring. Thus, when the gun fired and recoiled, the ram was forced back
on to the cylinder, increasing the air pressure. About 70% of the recoil shock was
taken by an oil-filled piston-and-cylinder arrangement beneath the cradle and the
recuperator absorbed the remainder. When the gun had been brought to rest in recoil,
the increased air pressure in the recuperator forced it back to its fully 'run-out' position.
The small cylinder at the rear side of the balance weight assembly maintained a liquid
pressure in the recuperator gland to prevent air leaks. On top of each cradle extension,
two changeover levers can be seen. In one position, they set a cam so that the breech
would open automatically on run-out, and this operation—known as 'semi-automatic'
—was the normal method of firing. As the breech opened, it ejected the empty
cartridge case on to the deck. At the opposite end of its quadrant, the lever held the cam
clear and the breech then had to be opened manually after each round had been fired.
Immediately below the SA lever, the breech mechanism lever can just be seen in its
housed position. It contained a heavy coil spring which was compressed by the SA
gear and which, in turn, closed the breech as soon as the round had been rammed into
the chamber. This arrangement relieved the breech-worker of considerable effort,
allowing him to concentrate on closing his firing circuit contactor as soon as the gun
was loaded. He is the rating inside the gunshield, and holds what looks like an
operating lever, but which was merely a support. The loading tray is ready, and the
tray-worker is about to push it over into line with the gun bore, and then ram the
round. Behind him, the right gun-loading numbers stand ready with a fresh shell and
cartridge, while on the far side the communications number wears a headset. Notice
the catch-nets, rolled up in rear of the balance weights. These arrested the empty cases
when they were ejected at low angles of elevation, but were usually lashed out of the
way during high-angle firing (IWM).

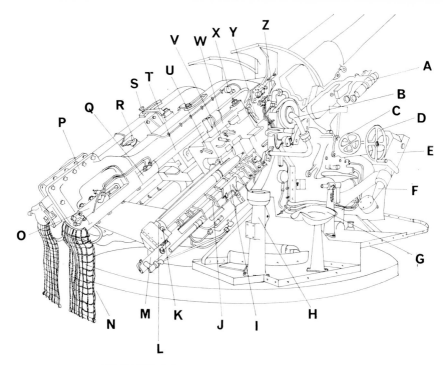

4·7-INCH CP TWIN MK XIX MOUNTING

(A) Trainer's monocular sight.   (B) Hydraulic exhaust take-off from elevating structure.   (C) Trainer's power handwheel.   (D) Trainer's hand drive.   (E) Training receiver.   (F) Drive to training receiver mechanical pointer.   (G) Fuze setter's seat. (H) Fuze setting pedestal.   (I) Loading tray unlocking palm lever.   (J) Loading tray. (K) Hand rammer head.   (L) Power rammer head.   (M) Rammer cylinder.   (N) Spent cartridge catch net.   (O) Intensifier, connected to recuperator cylinder gland. (P) Balance weights.   (Q) Recuperator cylinder.   (R) Loading light.   (S) Semi-automatic/quick fire changeover lever.   (T) Recuperator ram.   (U) Breech mechanism lever locking lever.   (V) Safe fire lever.   (W) Breech mechanism lever.   (X) Rounds fired counter.   (Y) Breech worker's percussion firing hand-grip.   (9) Firing circuit interceptor.

DATA

All-up weight:	*25·5 tons approx.*
Max. elevation:	*40 degrees*
Max. depression:	*10 degrees*
Max. training arc:	*320 degrees*
Max. speeds in power:	*10 degrees/second*

2 × 4·7-inch Mk XII or Mk XII guns:*
12 rounds per minute per gun (power ramming)
Max. effective surface range: 17,000 yards

through a swivel connection in the central pivot of the mounting for the hydraulic training and elevation engines. In power, a maximum speed of 10° per second was possible in both motions, and change-clutches were provided to enable the layer and trainer to control the mounting in emergency by hand, from separate handwheels.

There were further swivel connections on each trunnion. Pressure oil was led through the left trunnion for the power rammers in the loading trays, and exhaust oil left the elevating portion through the right-hand axis.

The combined weight of the 50lb shell and its 35lb cartridge was more than

A quadruple pompom, 2-pdr Mk VII shown on a destroyer. The smartly turned out crew are either posed or at drill, for in action they would wear overalls and anti-flash gear as shown on page 19. (IWM).

could be conveniently man-handled, so the ammunition was separated into two components. The loading tray was moved into line with the breech by hand, both the round and its charge being power-rammed together by the operation of a control lever. An independent hand-rammer was fitted as a secondary method of loading. With a fully trained crew, under 'power' conditions, a rate of fire of 12 r.p.m. per gun could be achieved.

The mountings had a training arc of approximately 320° centred about zero for the forward guns and 180° for 'X' and 'Y'. Normally, aiming was by the layer and trainer 'matching pointers' on their respective receivers in power—or in hand, if power failed—but conventional gunsight telescopes were also fitted, set by a geared sight drive on the left-hand side. Sighting ports were cut in the gun shield in the usual way, and were sealed in the non-action state by hinged doors which opened outwards.

On the whole, the twin Mk XIX was quite a good mounting but, like the earlier singles, its maximum elevation was only 40°, so in this respect it was no improvement on the earlier models.

The results of this limitation are seen on page 32 which shows the effective elevation of several mountings against arbitrary aircraft courses. The 'blind spots' created by the low evelation limit are so apparent as to need no further elaboration.

The next calibre in the 'as first fitted' armament was that of the quad 2-pdr pompom in which much confidence was placed before the war. Again the 'Tribals' can claim a first in introducing this as a destroyer fitting.

The earliest type was the 'M' Mk VII, itself a junior size model of the contemporary eight-barrelled version developed for capital ships. In the preliminary drafts of the 'Tribal' design it had been hoped, in fact, to fit the big eight-barrelled 'Chicago piano' mount, but this was ruled out for top-weight reasons.

The 'M' Mk VII's four barrels were staggered in pairs to create space for their ammunition trays. The gun-feed mechanism was fearfully complex, precluding its detailed explanation in this book, but if the reader can visualize the valve

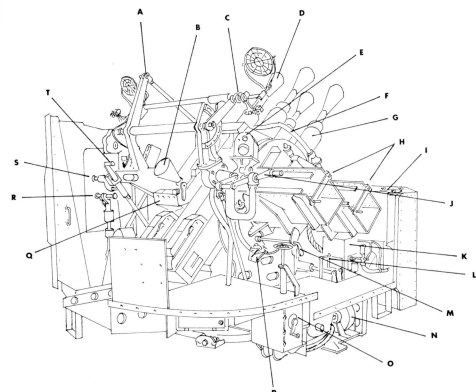

QUADRUPLE 2-PDR MK VII* (P) MOUNTING

(A) Sight linkage. (B) Water cooling filling position. (C) Backsight, with blank outer eyepieces. (D) Flame guard. (E) Trainer receiver. (F) Water-cooling pipe. (G) Water jacket. (H) Ammunition trays, each holding 112 rounds. (I) Circulating water tank. (J) Training hand-cranks. (K) Oil tank. (L) Safety firing gear. (M) Firing interruptor lever. (N) Hydraulic training motor. (O) Pump motor starter. (P) Elevation and depression buffer. (Q) Loading indication lamp box. (R) Power joystick. (S) Elevation hand-cranks. (T) Firing hand-cranks.

DATA

All-up weight:	*11 tons approx.*
Max. elevation:	*80 degrees*
Max. depression:	*10 degrees*
Max. training arc:	*710 degrees*
Max. speed in power:	*25 degrees/second*

4 × 2-pdr Mk VIII guns:
  98 rounds per minute per gun
  Max. effective surface range: 3,800 yards

Notes

This model replaced the earlier 'M' Mk VII, which was hand-worked only. For clarity, drawing omits the right rear gunshield.

gear of a steam locomotive at high speed, he will have a fair idea of the movement of the links and levers within the gun body. Each barrel delivered about 100 rounds per minute and each gun tray held 112 rounds in an articulated steel belt. Ammunition was made up in sections of 14 rounds and these could be added to the *in-situ* belt as it disappeared (like a demented caterpillar) into the gun body.

Pompoms—like Gatlings—suffered from a tendency to jam and often needed a

The famous 'quad' pompom in this photo is sited immediately abaft the funnel of a later class of destroyer, as evidenced by the siren on the right and the davit head in the foreground. When this was taken in the early part of the war, flame guards had already been fitted to the muzzles, but splinter shields had not. Both the layer and the trainer have to adopt an uncomfortable position in order to aim at this high angle of elevation, but the centre member of the gun's crew, who only mans the firing gear hand-cranks, is more fortunate. Two loading numbers are attaching a new belt of 14 rounds into one of the feed trays (IWM).

This pompom has only too clearly been in action, judging by the mixed heap of empty cases and articulated belt links on the deck. The gun's crew have a welcome breather and a quick smoke between attacks and, although they are relaxed here, will be galvanized into action at the order 'Stand to'. The ratings in the background are probably from the off-watch engine room department and are typically clad, but the pompom crew have 'anti-flash' hoods and gloves to protect them from burns (IWM).

19

ABOVE: HMS Bedouin *in October 1941. The view aft shows the Vickers multiple machine gun mount with ammunition drums in place. Further aft the pompom mount is just visible with its ammunition trays filled. The crew appear to be at 'Cruising Stations' with only token manning of the armament. Details to note are the steam pipes on the funnel, the siren, and the extensive use of plastic splinter padding on the 'bandstands'. Far aft the depth charge launcher is loaded and some 'reloads' are receiving attention on deck. OPPOSITE, TOP: On the bridge of* Eskimo *at 'Cruising Stations', March 1942. Air defence lookouts are closed up and the captain (beret and pipe) and officer of the watch (cap) are leaning against the binnacle. Note the rolled canvas screen (far left) which sealed off the navigator's chart table at night and allowed the chart to be illuminated. OPPOSITE: Midshipman of the watch,* Ashanti, *December 1941, with the duty watch of signalmen behind him. The main gyro compass repeater is to the right of the picture with voice-pipes to the wheelhouse and captain's sea cabin, and the alarm gong in front. Behind the midshipman is the binnacle with the magnetic compass (MoD).*

The pronounced 'stagger' of the barrels of the quadruple Vickers 0·5-inch machine-gun mounting is clearly shown here. The layer has a curved body-rest and is using both hands on his elevating handwheel. The trainer, on the right, could either push the mounting around or use his geared hand-drive. Points to notice are the fluted water-jackets on the guns; the conical flame guards on the muzzles; the drums of belt ammunition; and the 'ear-defenders' worn by the crew. The 'Officer of the Quarters' is in Tropical rig and this shot was probably taken in the Mediterranean (IWM).

well-directed clout with a wooden mallet to keep them going. Given their head, however—and jams permitting—they could put up a hail of contact-fuze projectiles, and it must have been daunting to fly towards them even when they were badly aimed.

The first mounting was handworked in elevation and training by the usual style of hand-cranks, with a third crank actuating the firing gear. The firing arrangements were soon modified for an electric motor drive, and later the whole mounting was adapted for complete power control, but the most apparent outward changes were the addition of a splinter shield to the mounting, and the fitting of flame guards to the gun muzzles.

Space could never be found in destroyers for a Pompom Director, which meant that the mounting was always aimed locally, and this detracted from its efficiency against fast aircraft targets. As a weapon, the 2-pdr was outclassed by the 40mm Bofors, but was a wonderful morale booster. It fired so much, so fast, and so noisily, that one felt it *must* be effective—and it could indeed decimate enemy coastal forces at close range.

The popularity of the 2-pdr gun waxed and waned over the years. In early destroyers—like the 'Vs' and 'Ws' of World War I for example, where it was fitted singly—it constituted the only effective anti-aircraft weapon, but in later classes it was replaced by a quadruple 0·5-inch Vickers machine-gun mounting. As we have seen, it then re-appeared in the quadruple mount, and finally towards the end of the Second World War, it came back as a 'single' in a power-operated, lightweight mounting. In this form it was fitted to several of the 'Z' class destroyers as well as the earliest 'Battles'.

Quite what advantage a quad machine-gun had over a 2-pdr single is not clear. Certainly its range was less and the destructive power of the machine-gun

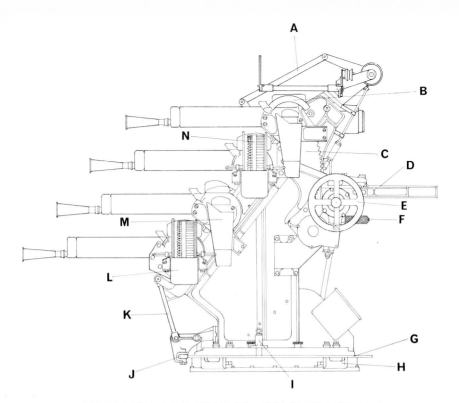

QUADRUPLE 0·5-INCH 'M' MK III MOUNTING

(A) Sight linkage. (B) Elevation scale. (C) Elevation arc connected No. 2 gun; all guns connected by parallel linkage. (D) Layer's body rest. (E) Elevating handwheel. (F) Training clutch lever. (G) Safety firing cam rail. (H) Mounting jumping clip. (I) Housing locking bolt. (J) Cam roller follower. (K) Safety firing linkage. (L) Guard tray under ammunition drum. (M) Spent cartridge tray. (N) Ammunition drum.

DATA

All-up weight:	*1·3 tons approx.*
Max. elevation:	*80 degrees*
Max. depression:	*10 degrees*
Max. training arc:	*Continuous*

4 × Vickers machine-guns, 0·5-inch, Mk III:
  700 rounds per minute per gun
  Max. effective surface range: 1,500 yards approx.

bullet was poorer. So far as the 'Tribals' were concerned, one might feel that the ammunition arrangements would have been somewhat easier if all the close-range weapons had been of the same calibre. But it may be that the Naval Staff preferred the 'shot-gun' effect of four machine-guns, which effect was deliberately increased by a designed misalignment between the individual barrels, giving four diverging trajectories.

In this weapon the barrels were mounted vertically above each other and were staggered backwards in the vertical plane to give access to the ammunition arrangements.

The gun mechanism was very similar to that of the 2-pdr (both were designed by Vickers) and the rate of fire was about 700 rounds per minute per gun. Again, the ammunition was contained in belts, but these were arranged

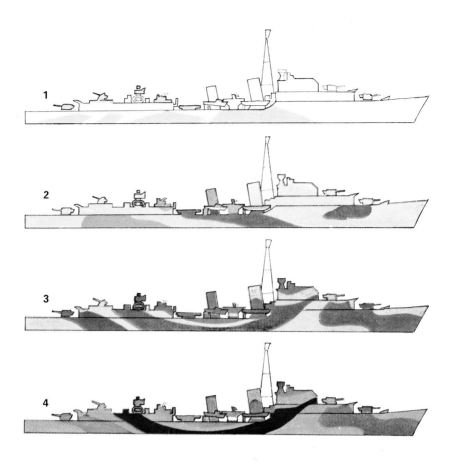

Fig 1
Western Approaches Scheme. There were several variations of this, including a long, shallow sloping panel starting from the forefoot. Very pale green was used initially, but there was a wartime shortage of green pigment and in about 1943 pale blue was substituted.

Figs 2, 3 and 4
Admiralty Disruptive Schemes. Light, Intermediate, and Dark, respectively

Pendant numbers were usually painted to contrast with the camouflage background, as can be seen on the photograph of *Ashanti* (page 46).

The disruptive schemes are not intended to portray a particular ship, but show the proportions of tones which varied in pattern. Often, ships had different patterns to port and starboard, but maintained the same *proportions* of tone on each side.

Decks were painted to conform with the general scheme, thus:

Figs 1 and 5	Light grey
Figs 2, 6, 7 and 10	Mid grey
Figs 3 and 8	Dark grey
Figs 4 and 9	Black

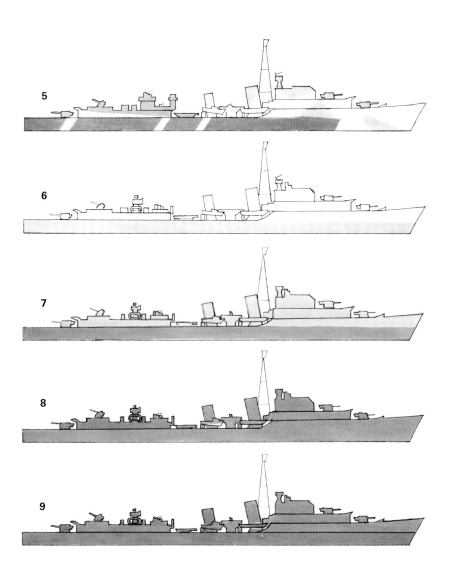

Fig 5
Special Home Fleet Destroyers Pattern.
*In use 1943-44. Adopted by RCN units and
some surviving RN 'Tribals'.*
Figs 6, 7, 8 and 9
Simplified Schemes. *Corresponding to Figs
1, 2, 3 and 4. These seem to have been favoured
in the Mediterranean theatre. The Fig 9 main
hull tone approximated to the pre-war Home
Fleet dark grey.*

around drums rather than 'concertina-ed' in trays. Aiming was by open 'cartwheel' sight, and few modifications were made during the Second World War other than the addition of a small splinter shield. As soon as the 20mm Oerlikon gun became available, the already obsolescent 0·5-inch machine-guns were removed and were replaced by either single or twin Oerlikon mountings.

FIRE CONTROL

The 'Tribals' retained the existing surface fire control arrangements of earlier classes. There was a Destroyer DCT on the bridge containing a gyro-stabilized sight and seats for the crew of five or six. The DCT transmitted data to a mechanical computer known as the Admiralty Fire Control Clock, which by a sequence of specially designed cams and similar devices, calculated the correct elevation and training for the guns. A bank of electrical transmitters conveyed these angles to the elevation and training receivers at the guns.

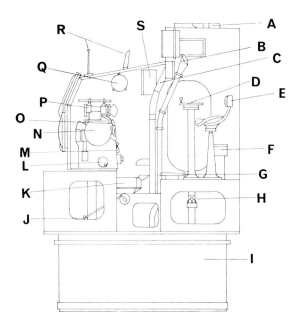

DESTROYER DIRECTOR CONTROL TOWER

(A) Lookout hatch. (B) Voice pipe to transmitting station. (C) Voice pipe to captain and R/F director. (D) Auxilliary training handwheel. (E) Rate officer's seat. (F) Gyro bearing indicator. (G) Director gyro sight operator's seat. (H) Dog-clutch in training drive. (I) Fixed pedestal. (J) Pedal-firing gear. (K) Layer's seat. (L) Elevation handwheel. (M) Gyro adjustment. (N) Type 'H' gyro director sight. (O) Layer's eyepiece of stabilized sight. (P) Layer's unstabilized binocular sight. (Q) Fire gong. (R) Open sight. (S) Gun ready lamp box.

DATA

All-up weight:	*1·9 tons approx.*
Max. elevation:	*40 degrees*
Max. training arc:	*440 degrees*
Crew:	*Control Officer, Rate Officer, Layer, Trainer, Gyro Adjustment Operator, Cross-level Operator*

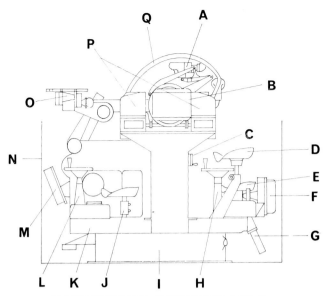

RANGEFINDER DIRECTOR MK II

(A) Control officer's binoculars. (B) Rangefinder. (C) Rangeworking handwheel. (D) Control officer's seat. (E) Rangetaker's seat. (F) Bearing receiver. (G) Rangetaker's seat adjustment. (H) Control officer's auxilliary training handwheel. (I) Fixed pedestal. (J) Trainer's seat. (K) Revolving structure. (L) Trainer's handwheel. (M) Bearing indicator. (N) Fixed windshield. (O) Trainer's binocular sight. (P) Anti-vibration mounting for rangefinder. (Q) Director cover support frame.

DATA

All-up weight:	1·5 tons approx.
Max. elevation:	50 (later 80) degrees
Max. training arc:	720 degrees

Notes

The director could be manned by a reduced crew—rangetaker and trainer—so, to keep the structure balanced, the trainer's and layer's seats were transposed from the usual arrangement.

An improved model, the Mk II (W), had a windscreen attached to the rotating structure and a Radar Type 285 'fishbone' aerial array set above the director rear.

Oddly, the rangefinder working in conjunction with the DCT in destroyers, had always been mounted separately, instead of being in the DCT itself. This improvement was first effected in the 'export' destroyers for Brazil (later appropriated by the Admiralty at the commencement of hostilities), but it was not until the 'L' class that a combined Destroyer DCT and rangefinder came into service in the Royal Navy—a refinement abandoned in the War Emergency classes. Yet another 'Tribal' 'first' lay in the fact that they introduced an AA predictor to destroyer classes. Hindered by the complication of a series of Naval Limitation treaties after the Great War, and unable to extract sufficient funds from the Treasury for development of an accurate system, the Admiralty were forced to accept a more elementary calculator.

This was another mechanical device employing a similar standard of gears and cams to those of the AFCC, but arranged to solve the three-dimensional problem of engaging an aircraft target. The unit, called the Fuze Keeping Clock, calculated the 'aim-off' necessary for the shell trajectory to pass through the expected position of the target, and added this to the Director's positional transmission to the gun receivers. The calculator's name derived from the fact

ABOVE: This bridge scene is believed to be aboard HMS Afridi early in 1940 and shows the ships' officers, and the commanding officer, Captain (later Admiral of the Fleet Sir) Philip Vian, wearing duffel coat on right. The picture is taken from the top of the DCT. Note the twin and single Lewis gun mounts which were later discarded, being of limited value against fast aircraft. In early 1940, Vian transfered to Cossack when Afridi was under repair and commanded Cossack at the time of the Altmark incident. BELOW: Right aft aboard Ashanti, showing the ready-use 4·7 inch rounds for 'Y' mounting, ready-use depth charges, and the usual dan-buoy and smoke floats (MoD).

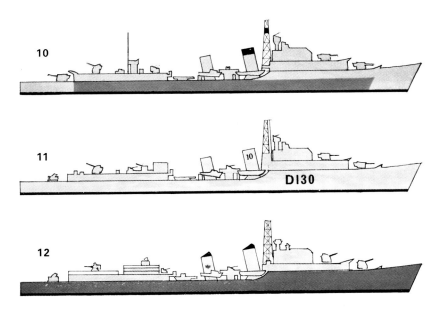

Fig 10
Standard Pattern. In 1944, the disruptive schemes were abandoned and a standard pattern was produced. Tartar *is shown in the European summer and general foreign stations shades. The European winter shades were one tone lighter in each case. Note that the black boot-tapping reappeared, whereas in early schemes, it was painted over to the load waterline.*

Fig 11
Royal Australian Navy, post-war. This tone corresponded approximately to the pre-war Mediterranean light grey.

Fig 12
Royal Canadian Navy, post-war. In the late 1950s the dark hull shade was abandoned in favour of overall light grey.

For deck colour detail see note on page 24.

A typical view off Malta, with local 'dghaisas' in the foreground, and Maori proceeding to sea beyond. She spent rather longer at Malta than most for she was bombed in harbour in 1942, and remained on the bottom until 1945, when she was salved and scuttled (A. & J. Pavia).

that it also predicted the setting of the time fuze for the AA shell nosecap, so that it would explode in the sky at the correct point in its flight.

The 'FKC' had several limitations. It could not produce an accurate solution if the target speed exceeded 250 knots and made the assumption that the aircraft course, height and speed would remain unchanged. Nevertheless, it was better than nothing, and remained in service throughout the war.

In this AA system, the simple rangefinder abaft the DCT was replaced by a Rangefinder-Director. The Mk I (Prototype) had been fitted—with the prototype FKC—in the sloop *Fleetwood*, and the Mk II was ready for the new destroyers. It was an open mounting carrying a rangefinder as before, but had a crew of four—Rangetaker, Layer, Trainer and Control Officer. All except the rangetaker, had binocular sights which elevated together from a geared elevation drive, with a take-off to keep the rangefinder in coincidence with them to a maximum of 80°. The trainer had a two-speed geared drive—slow for tracking and fast for slewing—which was duplicated by an auxiliary training handwheel for the Control Officer.

In AA fire, the Rangefinder-Director assumed control of aiming and firing, and the DCT was not used. In surface fire, however, the RF/D was manned by a reduced crew and then functioned solely as a rangefinder. It was surrounded by a fixed drum-shaped wind shield on the platform base, with the rangefinder 'arms' just clear of the rim. The Control Officer had to oscillate between each director, depending upon the type of engagement; an inconvenient arrangement.

ANTI-SUBMARINE WEAPONS
The early practice of building alternate flotillas for A/S and mine-sweeping duties had long ceased, and in the 'Tribals' no provision was made for the 'Two Speed Destroyer Sweep'. There was, in any case, little space available on the quarterdeck, but a single overstern rack for three depth charges was positioned on the centre line, with stowages for nine reloads. A depth charge

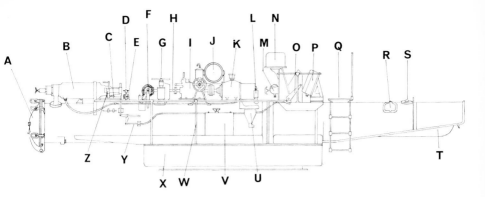

21-INCH QUADRUPLE TORPEDO TUBE MOUNTING

(A) Rear door. (B) Explosion chamber. (C) Set gyro angle. (D) Set torpedo speed. (E) Set pattern run (30° zig-zag course). (F) Hand training drive. (G) Set depth. (H) Training drive shaft. (I) Variable speed unit. (J) Training receiver. (K) Electric training motor. (L) Cordite gas-operated top stop. (M) Tube ready switch. (N) Local torpedo sight. (O) Firing lever (one for each tube). (P) Tube order receiver. (Q) Platform across tubes. (R) Access to torpedo pistol. (S) Access to depth and roll recorder (practice torpedoes only). (T) 21-inch Mk IX torpedo, 11,000 yards range at 40 knots. (U) Tube operator's seat. (V) Training motor starter. (W) Guard rails. (X) Cover over training rollers. (Y) Cable from firing lever. (Z) Breech.

thrower was set unusually high on each side of the superstructure abreast the tripod main mast, again with adjacent reload stowages.

TORPEDO ARMAMENT

The offensive power of the ships was completed by one quadruple torpedo mounting. A pentad (or five-fold) mounting was available at the time, but was probably ruled out for top-weight reasons. British destroyers carried no torpedo reloads, but usually had a small workshop on the upper deck where the delicate torpedo gyros were stowed: and limited maintenance on the 'fish' could be carried out on board. With the rear door of a tube hinged down and the torpedo partially withdrawn to the rear, some basic maintenance could be carried out, but the engine could not be test-run because it relied on surrounding sea water to keep it cool. When the torpedo was in position in the tube its external setting shafts were aligned to spring-loaded handles which allowed depth and speed to be set immediately before firing. In the rear of each tube there was a cylindrical impulse chamber with a simple breech for a cordite cartridge and, when fired, the expanding gases thrust the torpedo forwards at a comparatively low velocity. A trigger started the engine and ran up the air-driven gyro. This kept the 'fish' on course by controlling the vertical rudders, while a hydrostatic device controlled the depth through the horizontal rudders.

In destroyers the tubes were always fired at 90° to the fore-and-aft line, so there was no need for a 'follow the pointer' control other than an indication of the firing beam. This was shown on a simple training receiver, the tubes being traversed either by hand-cranks or by an electric motor drive. Normal control was from the Torpedo Sights on each side of the bridge, and the firing ship usually turned in an arc away from the target as the torpedoes were launched, so that there was a 'spread' in their tracks.

Under some attack circumstances it became necessary to fire the torpedoes on a course other than broadside to the ship, and this was achieved, not by

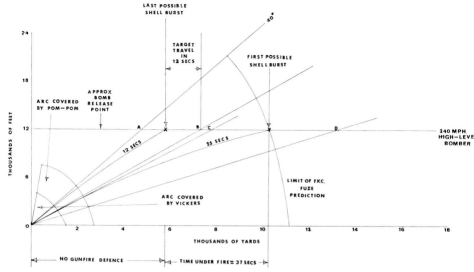

DIAGRAM OF HIGH-LEVEL BOMBER ATTACK

'O' is own ship; 'OD' is director line of sight to target; 'DY' is target travel in 25 seconds; and 'OC' is gun elevation to produce 25-second trajectory 'OY'.

Because 'Y' is on the outer limit of the FKC prediction, it becomes the first possible shell burst. Similarly, 'OA' is maximum gun elevation and gives 12-second trajectory 'OX'. 'XB' is target travel in 12 seconds, so 'OB' is director line of sight when last gun fires; and 'X' is the last possible shell burst.

'XY' becomes the time under fire, and no trajectory can pass through a point nearer than 'X' at this particular target height.

This problem was relieved to some extent when the twin 4-inch was fitted, because its maximum elevation allowed the target to be engaged to the bomb release point; but only comparatively low-level targets could be effectively engaged by the close-range weapons.

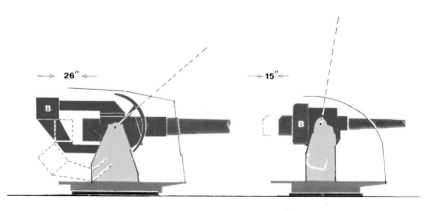

BASIC MOUNTING CONSTRUCTION

Left: Twin 4·7-inch   Right: Twin 4-inch.
Working recoil shown in inches.
Red: Elevating, non-recoiling structure.
Blue: Elevating, recoiling structure.
Yellow: Trunnion supports.
Green: Training base.
Purple: Deck ring.
'B':   Balance weight.

training the tubes, but by pre-setting the gyro, which again could be carried out by a hand-wheel on the tube itself. The torpedo was then launched in the usual way, but turned through the angle set after it had entered the water.

Later mountings had a control cupola for local control, but the quads on the RN 'Tribals' merely had a seat on the right-hand side of the platform with a secondary torpedo sight close to the four 'signal box' style firing levers. All the ships retained their tubes for the duration of their working lives.

Tartar *displaying the white band of the 6th Flotilla, which she is wearing in 1940, as she passes under the 6-inch guns of a friendly cruiser in the Firth of Forth. In June 1944 she was damaged in an action off Cherbourg against German surface vessels. They were the only force capable of challenging the impending invasion, and were duly despatched. In this very well lit picture the torpedo tubes and the separate DCT and R/FD can all be easily distinguished. (IWM).*

Chapter 3:
Wartime Changes

THE 12 RN vessels which succumbed were lost between April 1940, when *Gurkha* was sunk off Norway, and September 1942, when *Zulu*, *Sikh* and *Somali* all went to the bottom. The full extent of wartime modifications were obviously not carried out on all ships and, in general, the longer they survived, the better equipped they emerged from refit.

NEW GUN MOUNTINGS
An early change came with the replacement of the twin 4·7 in 'X' position by a twin 4-inch Mk XIX. We have seen how limited were the AA capabilities of the designed armament, and this was improved to some extent by the inclusion of the AA mounting—an efficient weapon with a maximum elevation of 80°. The modifications made to the fire control to embrace the dissimilar calibres will be discussed in due course.

THE 4-INCH TWIN MK XIX MOUNTING
In 1933 a development contract was placed for a twin 4-inch HA mounting to replace the existing single gun, and the new weapon began to enter service in 1937, initially as secondary armament on cruisers and on some refitted

Tartar was the fourth 'Tribal' to go right through the war and was the first to be scrapped. The last four ships were formed up into the 10th Flotilla and Tartar—the Leader—*was probably on her way home from the East Indies when this picture was taken in 1945. She went back to Devonport—her home port—to become an administration centre, before she de-equipped for scrapping. In this view all the wartime changes described in this chapter can be seen—twin 4-inch mount in 'X' position, Oerlikons replacing machine guns, added radar, and a lattice mast. (A. & J. Pavia).*

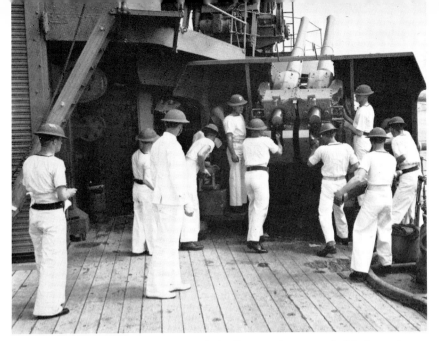

This photo has been included to show the loading procedure on a twin 4-inch mount, although, of course, the ship is not a 'Tribal'. The right-hand loader has just beaten the left, for his breech has closed under the action of its spring, pushing his clenched fist upwards. The left loader is in the final movement of ramming his round home. Padded 'knuckle-dusters' are worn by the loading numbers to protect their fingers. The two ratings facing inwards are the breech workers, who make their firing circuit contactor as soon as their gun is loaded, and the loading number is clear of the gun's recoil. The next pair of rounds are being held on the fuze-setting trays while their fuze nose settings are applied and another loading number on each side forms a queue. A CPO—who is very probably a gunner's mate—is in overall charge of the drill, which is being timed by the rating holding a stop-watch in the rear (IWM).

capital ships.

Referring to page 32 we can see that it was arranged quite differently from the contemporary 4·7-inch guns. The trunnion axis was proportionately higher and the balance weight, made necessary by pushing the breech end towards the elevating axis, was attached to the recoiling part of the gun, immediately in front of the breech rings. No loading trays were fitted and the two breech blocks opened vertically downwards.

Because it was hand-loaded it used 'fixed' ammunition—ie, combined shell and cartridge—whose all-up 55lb was an acceptable weight for the loading numbers in the gun's crew to handle. It should be noted that they loaded from a position directly behind the gun.

The trunnion height was arranged to suit the maximum elevation in full recoil and this made loading rather awkward at low elevations—when, of course, the breech end was comparatively high. At the same time it was literally an uphill task to load the guns at very high elevations. Nevertheless this could be done, and in any case a pre-loaded gun could be fired at 80°. Remembering that the total weight of the 4·7-inch shell and cartridge made it necessary to separate them, we see the immediate difference in the design of the 4·7-inch mounting. Although the breech is close to the trunnion, the gun needs a loading tray and rammer, which immediately restricts the maximum

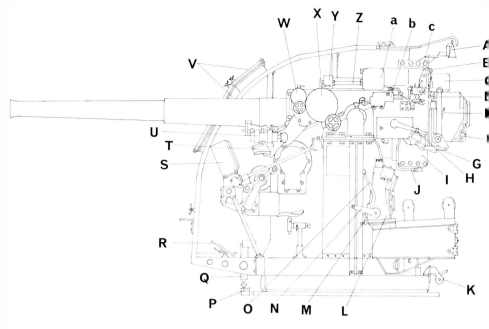

4-INCH HA TWIN MK XIX MOUNTING

(A) Loading lamp.   (B) Percussion firing lever.   (C) Recuperator cylinder.
(D) Breech mechanism lever. (E) Breech mechanism lever locking lever. (F) Safe/
fire lever. (G) Semi-automatic gear link. (H) Semi-automatic/quick fire changeover
lever. (I) Balance weight. (J) Recoil cylinder compensating pipe. (K) Training
buffer. (L) Fuze-setting machine, Mk II. (M) Follow fuze number. (N) Fuze-setting
handle. (O) Ejector lever. (P) Safety firing cam. (Q) Safety firing roller follower.
(R) Layer's footrest.   (S) Elevation receiver.   (T) Star shell datum spirit level.
(U) Layer's monocular. (V) Sighting ports. (W) Deflection dial. (X) Range dial.
(Y) Recuperator ram cross-head.   (Z) Cross-head tie-rod.   (a) Recoil cylinder
compensating tank. (b) Intensifier. (c) Interceptor.

DATA

All-up weight:	14 tons approx.
Max. elevation:	80 degrees
Max. depression:	10 degrees
Max. training arc:	340 degrees
2 × 4-inch Mk XVI guns:	
Max. effective surface range:	18,000 yards

Notes

Later modifications included:
  (a) Extension of gunshield to rear.
  (b) Replacement of Mk II by Mk V fuze-setting machines.
  (c) Addition of electric powered elevation and training in association with
      Remote Power Control.

elevation; and balancing is achieved by a weight supported from a beam
projecting rearwards from the cradle. The tray is loaded from the *side* and the
trunnion height makes it easy to load at all elevations within its limits.

It follows that neither design could fulfil a true 'dual-purpose' requirement,
though the twin 4-inch was useable in this rôle and became the main armament
of smaller ships—for example the 'Hunt' class escort destroyers. Only its lesser
destructive power (compared with the 4·7-inch projectile) prevented it from
becoming the standard destroyer gun, although both the post-war 'Weapon'
class and the Type 15 and 16 A/S frigates adopted it as their main armament—

as did the fast minelayers.

The other major weapon change was the replacement of the multiple Vickers guns by Oerlikons, and the addition of similar guns on the bridge wings. The latter position offered so many advantages that it is curious it was not adopted from the design stage. Abreast the bridge, a close-range gun had good height; the best possible arcs of fire for a 'sided' mounting; was clear of the boats; and provided almost personal protection for those closed-up on the open bridge. It is, of course, true to say that ·303-inch machine-guns were sometimes mounted abreast the bridge, but more in hope than expectation of hitting a target.

THE 20mm OERLIKON AND THE 40mm BOFORS

The Oerlikon gun did not become available until about the middle of 1941, and it was then fitted to the surviving 'Tribal' ships when opportunity offered, at first supplementing the multiple machine-guns and finally replacing them.

Like the Bofors, the weapon was available well before the war, but both

The aimer of this single 20mm Oerlikon mounting wears the badge of an AA specialist and is well clad in gloves and sheepskin jacket, which may indicate an Arctic convoy. The mounting pedestal is surrounded by a circular tier of platforms to suit the elevation of the gun; and the firing arcs are restricted by the tubular steel rails, shaped to prevent the gun from firing into the ship's structure. The gun is cocked, but this is a 'posed' photograph, because no magazine is fitted. Ready use ammunition is stowed in the lockers in the foreground, and a canvas bag is fitted below the gun-body to catch the ejected cases. This particular gun is fitted on the quarterdeck of an escort, whose overstern depth charge rails can be seen on the left (IWM).

SINGLE 20mm OERLIKON MOUNTING

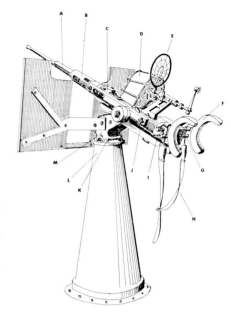

(A) Non-recoiling barrel. (B) Recoiling barrel spring casing. (C) Double-loading interlock. (D) 58-round magazine. (E) Foresight, with 300, 200 and 100 knot rings. (F) Shoulder rests. (G) Hand-grips. (H) Aimer's body-strap. (I) Trigger. (J) Cotter, connecting recoiling side plates to gun bolt. (K) Trunnion. (L) Fixed pedestal. (M) Training cradle.

guns were regarded with suspicion, not so much because they were foreign, but because of certain aspects of their design.

There had been serious accidents in the period of rapid development of modern guns in the 19th century, and from them 'Golden Rules' emerged. One was that the breech should be positively locked before the charge was detonated, and another was that in semi-automatic operation a sliding breech

TWIN 20mm OERLIKON MK V MOUNTING

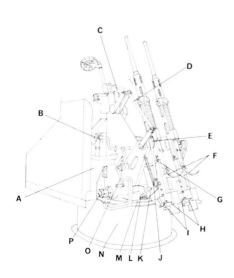

(A) Aimer's seat. (B) Normal/Emergency hydraulic changeover valve. (C) Sight bracket. (D) Sight linkage. (E) Safety firing interrupter cam, prevents (G) from moving on dangerous bearings. (F) Magazine catches. (G) Firing cam, lifted by firing cylinder. (H) Triggers. (I) Firing levers, connected by linkage to firing cam. (J) Interruptor mechanism spring. (K) Interruptor mechanism operating lever. (L) Operating lever roller. (M) Safety firing cam, cut to profile of ship's structure. (N) Fixed base. (O) Hand drive to emergency hydraulic pump. (P) Emergency pump.

DATA

All-up weight:	1 ton approx.
Max. elevation:	70 degrees
Max. depression:	10 degrees
Max. training arc:	Continuous all-round
Max. surface range:	6,250 yards at 45 degrees

Note
The sight bracket was later modified to take a US Mk 14 gyro gunsight.

The power-operated twin Oerlikon Mk V mounting. The guns are secured to an elevating support which projects backwards from the trunnions, so that the off-mounting loader can replace empty magazines as required. None are fitted in this photograph which shows the mounting under routine maintenance, with the Ordnance Artificer perched on the back-rest of the aimer's seat. Notice the linkage to the heavily built gyro-gunsight bracket, and the semi-circular platform for the loader. This 'sided' mounted had continuous all-round training and cam-operated interruptor gear to prevent it from firing into its own ship's structure. The hydraulic power unit, with its associated electric pump motor and starter, are mounted on an adjacent splinter screen. From this unit the oil pressure delivery and exhaust return pipes led to the mounting through a swivel joint in its base. In the event of a power failure, hydraulic pressure could be supplied from a hand pump on the mounting, worked by the loader. One of its hand-cranks can be seen above the left gun. Variants of this mounting were produced to carry a single 2-pdr pompom, or a single 40mm Bofors (the latter much favoured by the RCN) (Anthony Peters).

block should never open during recoil, but only during 'run out', when the energy of firing had been absorbed. Neither of the foreign guns conformed completely to these requirements. The Oerlikon had a comparatively simple 'pump action' cylindrical bolt which flew backwards and forwards taking rounds from the magazine and ramming them into the chamber. They were actually struck just before reaching the fully 'home' position, and in blowing backwards the bolt pulled out the empty case and ejected it vertically downwards. Meanwhile, the barrel springs were being compressed and in reasserting themselves, repeated the process as long as the trigger was pressed. It was largely through the personal efforts of Lord Louis Mountbatten that the gun was finally adopted and the story of its development is admirably told by Gerald Pawle in his fascinating book *The Secret War*.

The 40mm Bofors gun—advertisements for which first appeared in the 1935 edition of *Janes Fighing Ships*—had a more conventional breech mechanism. It employed a vertical sliding block of normal design, but it opened during recoil to eject the empty case. The advantage of this operating cycle lay in the fact that the chamber was emptied almost as soon as the gun fired, enabling it

A sombre picture of dawn—or perhaps dusk—action stations. This is the single Bofors Mk 7 mounting, developed from the twin Oerlikon; but unlike the earlier weapon it was completely self-contained, and its hydraulic power unit was carried on-mounting. Again, it had the 'emergency' hand-crank pump. On the loader's right is the 'letterbox' stowage for on-mounting ammunition; in front of him, but out of sight in this view, the aimer sat in a 'sports-car' style cab, controlling the mounting by a 'scooter' control unit. The RN 'Tribals' were too late to receive this mark of Bofors mounting but it was quite widely fitted in the Commonwealth ships (Anthony Peters).

to fire about 120 rounds per minute, 20% more than the pompom, and with better range. Unhappily it took much precious time to overcome the prejudices levelled against this most efficient gun.

ANTI-SUBMARINE WEAPONS

Study of photographs indicates that the D/C throwers abreast the main mast were not fitted to all ships, and they then relied solely on the overstern rail in A/S attacks.

As a class, the original 'Tribals' were never intended to carry an extensive anti-submarine armament, and none in any case, ever had more than two throwers. During the war, those with throwers dropped them one deck to the more usual level on the Iron Deck and their reloading was then effected by the standard six-charge parbuckle stowage.

The close proximity of 'Y' mounting to the stern precluded the four-thrower set-up so common in later destroyer classes; and it similarly restricted the size of the overstern charge-dropping trap-and-rails to a short section holding three. The ships were, therefore, only ever able to deliver the 'five pattern'

This splendid 1942 photograph of Punjabi *refuelling was taken from the cruiser* Kent. *The after funnel has not been cut down, but she has the 286 'bedstead' aerial at the main topmast head. Notice the relative sizes of the twin 4-inch and the twin 4·7 mount in 'Y' position; the short depth charge rail on the rounded stern; and that, sadly, the White Ensign is at half-mast. While she was escorting convoy PQ15 in May 1942 she was rammed and sunk in thick weather by the battleship* King George V. *As* Punjabi *foundered, her depth charges exploded and so damaged the capital ship that it was forced to return for repairs (IWM).*

attack, expending the three overstern charges, and one from each thrower, in a roughly cross-shaped drop. The moment of release was determined by the Asdic set in conjunction with its transducer, carried in a small retractable dome beneath the keel, and discharge was normally fully automatic. There were, however, the usual local firing arrangements both for the throwers and the overstern gear.

FIRE CONTROL CHANGES

The original model of R/F Director Mk II was fairly quickly replaced by a sub-model known as the Mk II (W). The suffix letter indicated that it had a windshield attached to the rotating structure and, when fitted, the earlier fixed drum shield was removed.

The principal function of the twin 4-inch in 'X' position was to provide barrage fire against dive bomber attacks above the 40° elevation limit of the main armament. However, to restrict it solely to these duties would have wasted its potential—since it was the standard anti-aircraft gun mounting—so it was linked to the existing HA fire control system. Fortunately—and oddly—its shell trajectory was very similar to that of the 4·7 inch, but its AA shell fuze setting was different, for a given range. A special unit was therefore added which converted the calculated 4·7-inch fuze setting to that for a 4-inch projectile and the HA mounting was used:

(a) In long-range control firing with the 4·7-inch armament up to 40° elevation against high-level targets.

(b) Alone against similar targets above 40° elevation.

(c) In barrage fire during dive bomber attacks.

Two other modifications altered the profile of the ships. Firstly, the after funnel was reduced in height and, secondly, the tall tripod main mast was dispensed with. The main roof radio aerials were then led to a 'goal post' frame on the after superstructure, and a pole mast topped by the HF D/F aerial replaced the tripod.

RADARS

At the outbreak of war in 1939, only the battleship *Rodney* and the cruiser *Sheffield* had radar—a 'warning' set based on the coastal radars in the South of England which were to play such a vital part in the Battle of Britain.

Radar development was in its infancy, and no small ship could tolerate the topweight of the early aerial arrays. However, the Royal Air Force had designed a small set for use in the air-to-surface reconnaissance rôle, which proved to be adaptable for ship fitting. It was known as Type 286M in the Royal Navy and had a fixed 'bedstead' aerial set on the fore topmast, facing forward. It could only give cover to about 60° on each side of the bow and, in any case, the ship had to be swung to obtain even an approximate target bearing. Its range and accuracy were weak, and altogether it was unpopular because it imposed such severe tactical limitations on the ship carrying it.

To improve the capabilities of Type 286M, the aerial was redesigned to rotate and so give the much needed all-round sweep. In this form the set was called 286P. It had been hoped that its range could also be improved, but despite the endeavours of the scientists ashore, this did not materialise. The problems of the Type 286 series really stemmed from the fact that the basic set had not been designed in the first instance for warship installation, and suffered accordingly. Nevertheless, even the limited range of Type 286 was better than nothing, and the 'Tribals' began to have its intricate 'bedstead' aerial fitted on their lofty fore topmasts in place of the existing lozenge-shaped D/F aerial.

The potential of radar for gunnery ranging was quickly appreciated and intensive onshore development began on sets specifically for this purpose. Prior to the radar era, target range (and height in AA fire) could only be established from the familiar optical instruments—always limited by the prevailing visibility.

A new radar—Type 285—was designed for lightweight HA directors and its 'fishbone' aerial array was to become a familiar sight throughout the Fleet.

As the 'Tribals' returned for refit and weapon improvement, their 'as fitted' Rangefinder Director Mk II was replaced by the better protected R/F Director Mk II (W) carrying the Type 285 radar aerial.

Meanwhile, general radar design was proceeding apace. In due course sets were produced for surface warning, air warning, height finding, interrogation and navigation, but sadly, few RN 'Tribals' were left to take advantage of them. Only the four survivors of the first desperate years of the war were comprehensively equipped, but the Commonwealth ships fared better.

The following radars were eventually fitted to surviving RN ships and

Commonwealth vessels:

RADAR SET TYPE	AERIAL	FUNCTION	LOCATION	REMARKS
286M	Fixed 'Bedstead'	Combined Sea/Air Warning	Fore top mast	First Radar set in RN Tribals
286P	Rotatable 'Bedstead'	Combined Sea/Air Warning	Fore top mast	
285	Yagi array ('Fishbone')	Gunnery	R/F Director Mk II (W) and III (W)	Most vessels during the war
271	Rotating 'cheese' (within 'lantern')	Surface warning	After superstructure	RCN *Haida* and *Huron* only
291	Rotating horizontal dipoles	Combined Sea/Air Warning	Fore top mast or pole mast head	Used mainly in the Air Warning rôle
276	Rotating 'cheese'	Combined Sea/Air Warning	Platform on fore side of fore mast	Interim set (aerial smaller than 293)
293	Rotating 'cheese'	Combined Sea/Air Warning	(1) Platform on fore side of fore mast (2) Platform on top of lattice masts	Became standard Gunnery Direction Set
242	Rotating 'Hayfork'	Aircraft Interrogator, Friend or Foe ('IFF')	(1) Independently on platform abaft fore top (2) Co-axial above 271 'lantern'	Replaced by 242 'Candelabra' aerial
242	Rotating 'Candelabra'	IFF	Platform abaft fore top	Trained, to interrogate suspicious echoes received by other Radars
253	Double wire cones, point-to-point	Surface ship interrogator	On short strut from fore mast	Non-rotatable
974	Small rotating 'Cheese'	Navigation	Platform on fore mast below 293	RAN only, on post-war modernisation
275	Twin 'Head-lamp' nacelles	Gunnery	Aerial supports on each side of Mk 6 Director	RCN *Athabaskan* (II) and *Cayuga* only
U.S. AN/SPG-34	Conical 'Dish'	Gunnery	(1) Elevating structure of U.S. 3 inch/50 cal. twin gun mount (2) Right-hand side of gun shield roof on twin 4 inch in 'B' position	RCN ships only (Not on 4 inch in *Athabaskan* and *Cayuga*)
High-Frequency Direction Finder ('HF D/F')	'Pyramid-on-Cube' frame	Detection of H/F radio transmissions	Fore top mast or pole mast aft	Surviving RN ships, *Zulu*, *Bataan*, *Warramunga*, *Athabascan* (I) and *Haida* only

Notes:
(1) Pre-war, RN ships had a lozenge-shaped Medium Frequency D/F aerial on the fore top mast. Most, later had the standard MF D/F aerial projecting from the bridge front.
(2) RCN ships had a non-standard HF D/F aerial on the fore top mast and USN warning radars with parabolic mesh aerials in place of RN sets.
(3) Most wartime ships had a TBS ('Talk between ships') radio pole aerial on the fore mast.
(4) Modernized Commonwealth ships had radio 'whip' aerials on the bridge side; on the funnel sides, and/or on the after superstructure.

Several wartime improvements had been implemented by 1941, when this photograph of Zulu *was taken in the Atlantic. The bridge wing sponsons have been stiffened to support single hand-worked 2-pdrs—a somewhat rare mounting in this class—but her quad Vickers between the funnels have not been changed. Here, her engines are going astern, and are thrusting a hissing mass of aerated water forward towards her lovely bow. She rises to the long Atlantic swell and her black boot-topping shows clear above the anti-fouling. When this occurred in heavy seas, ships often received jocular signals, such as 'Your slip is showing', and others quite unprintable (IWM).*

OTHER CHANGES

On all ships as they refitted the searchlight was removed from its platform but the platform itself was retained, because it carried the emergency steering position with its duplicate wheel and engine room telegraphs.

As we have seen, by September 1942 there were only four of these splendid ships left (if one discounts *Maori* which settled on the bottom in Valetta, Malta, after being damaged in an air attack) and the survivors received further modifications. A lattice foremast replaced the old tripod, up-to-date radars were fitted, and powered twin 20mm Oerlikons were mounted in place of, or in addition to, the existing singles.

Many more changes than these took place on the Commonwealth 'Tribals' but these involve a separate development history and details are given in Chapter 5 which deals with these vessels.

Chapter 4:
A Pictorial Record of
Royal Navy 'Tribals'

EXAMPLES of 'Tribal' class destroyer armament, fittings, and changes have been illustrated throughout the text. To complete the coverage of the British vessels, this section shows all of them at various stages in their service careers. Some ships are shown in camouflage and cross-reference to the colour pages will enable the reader to determine the colours in most cases. As far as space permits the pictures are shown chronologically though this is not possible in every case. Commonwealth 'Tribals' are all illustrated separately in Chapter 5.

Ashanti *was among the four surviving RN ships and her name is perpetuated in one of the present-day Type 81 frigates. This photograph was taken in July 1939, when she was painted in overall dark grey, with white pendant numbers and flotilla funnel band. The 'Tribals' were originally allocated Flag L superior, but this was changed in 1938. During the war* Ashanti *was an escort to Russian Convoy PQ 14, and towed her damaged sister* Somali *for eight hours before the latter foundered. Later, in the Mediterranean, she was again part of an escort force—this time of the 'Pedestal' convoy to Malta, which included the famous American tanker* Ohio *(P. A. Vicary).*

In 1940, the superior flag was again changed and Ashanti became G51. Here, she speeds past a rugged terrain and is heavily camouflaged in the Admiralty 'disruptive' scheme. The photograph dates from 1941 and shows a number of wartime modifications. Splinter shields have been added to the gundecks; the Rangefinder Director Mk II has been replaced by a Mk II (W) (with Radar Type 285); Warning Radar Type 286 is carried on the fore topmast; the after funnel has been reduced in height and the main mast removed completely. Notice the splinter shield added to the pompom, the 4-inch twin in 'X' position and the careful application of the camouflage, which leaves not only the pendant number in contrast, but also the flotilla band on the funnel (IWM).

This photograph of Bedouin was taken in 1942, only a few months before she was lost in June of that year. Operational requirements had prevented her from receiving the improvements enjoyed by some of her contemporaries and, even at this time, she still has her old R/F director and tripod main mast. The unusual arrangement of two whalers on the starboard side should be noted, but may have been a temporary measure. Bedouin suffered heavy shellfire damage from Italian cruisers and was finally despatched by a torpedo bomber (IWM).

Another member of the 1st (Tribal) Destroyer Flotilla was Gurkha, shown here off Malta in 1938, soon after she had commissioned at Devonport. Photographs of her are rare for she was the first of her class to be lost, succumbing to German bombs off Stavanger, Norway, in April 1940, a few months after she had sent U-53 to the bottom (A. & J. Pavia).

An interested crowd looks on as Cossack—then under the command of Captain Philip Vian—returns to Leith in February 1940 after rescuing the British prisoners held in Graf Spee's supply ship Altmark. No appreciable changes have been made since pre-war days except for the addition of splinter padding to her R/F director and also to the searchlight platform. Cossack was damaged and ran aground in the second battle of Narvik; attacked a German convoy in October 1940; and was Leader of the destroyer action against the Bismark. Torpedoed by a U-boat in the North Atlantic on October 23, 1941, she finally foundered four days later (IWM).

Maori entering Grand Harbour from what was quite probably her last operation before she was sunk. She was involved in the Bismark action and stopped to pick up survivors from the German battleship. In December 1941 she joined Sikh, Legion and the Dutch Isaac Sweers in the action which resulted in the sinking of the Italian cruisers Alberto di Giussano and Alberico da Barbirarie. Notice her dark hull, light upperworks, and the two red bands of the 2nd Flotilla (IWM).

47

In about 1942, Eskimo *was painted in the white/light blue 'Western Approaches' camouflage scheme. She was engaged in Arctic convoys to Russia, when doubtless the suitability of her name gave rise to ribald remarks. She refitted in 1943, became an Administration Ship in 1947, and was finally scrapped in 1949 (IWM).*

An early view of Mashona *on trials, wearing the Vickers House Flag. She commissioned at Chatham in March 1939 and was sunk by German bombers off Ireland in May 1941 (IWM).*

The camera angle makes Mashona *look incredibly long as she lies to a buoy at Portland in May 1939 during her 'work-up'. She was heavily engaged in the Norwegian campaign with a number of her sisters (P. A. Vicary).*

Matabele *was another of the Chatham-manned 'Tribals' and was one of the repeat group of nine. After the loss of* Afridi *in May 1940, Captain Vian transferred to* Cossack *and relieved Commander Sherbrooke who, in turn, assumed command of this ship. Here, she is painted in Home Fleet dark grey as she leaves Portsmouth in March 1939 (Wright & Logan).*

By 1941, Matabele *had had several wartime modifications incorporated. She was part of the escort of the first convoy to Russia (PQ1) in September 1941, but was sunk by a U-boat in the following year. Only two of her entire ship's company were saved—a grim reminder to others of the chances of survival in the icy waters (IWM).*

Mohawk, *built by Thornycroft of Southampton, was the only RN unit to be named after a North American Indian tribe—if one discounts the Eskimos. She is shown here in Southampton Water during her 1938 trials (IWM).*

Like all the first group of ships, Mohawk *was in the 1st (Tribal) Destroyer Flotilla and, in fact, spent most of her life in the Mediterranean. In April 1941 she was part of the 14th Flotilla and in action against an enemy convoy off the North African coast. All the convoy and two of its three escorts were sunk, but in her death throes one of the Italian warships discharged three torpedoes at* Mohawk, *two of which hit, sinking her with the loss of 41 lives (A. & J. Pavia).*

Nubian *entering Grand Harbour in 1939, with the battleship* Malaya *in the background. She was the second of the Southampton-built pair, and her first Captain remained in command from October 1938 until June 1942.* Nubian *was in action with* Mohawk *against the Italian convoy and was later damaged by bombs during the desperate days of Crete (A. & J. Pavia).*

Nubian *remained in the Mediterranean until 1943 and was then detached to join up with the Eastern Fleet. In this shot, dating from 1944, she is shown after having been extensively refitted. She has power twin Oerlikons on the bridge wings and another 'sided' pair on the after superstructure. Single Oerlikons have replaced the Vickers machine-guns between the funnels and her new lattice mast carries Radars 293, 291 and 242. Abaft the 'goalpost' frame for the main roof aerials is a pole mast for the HF/DF aerial. Notice the simple camouflage panel (P. A. Vicary).*

Malta said farewell to Nubian *in 1945. Here, she leaves Grand Harbour flying her paying-off pendant, with a war-damaged tanker beyond and Fort Ricasoli on her starboard bow. She had a very full career, which included the evacuation of Namsos in Norway, the battle of Matapan, and the bombardment of Salerno in 1943. Note that the blue camouflage panel shown in the previous pictures has been freshly painted out (A. & J. Pavia).*

Punjabi *lying to her starboard anchor off Portsmouth in May 1939. The 16ft 'skimming dish' is alongside the port gangway, having just been lowered by the torpedo davit (Wright & Logan).*

Sikh *was another member of the Mediterranean flotilla before the war. She was built on the Clyde at Alexander Stephen's yard, which also produced* Zulu. *This photo was taken in 1938, a month after she had commissioned at Chatham (Wright & Logan).*

Somali was one of the 'Tribals' initially fitted out as a Leader and already had a black band on her funnel in March 1939. Originally, she was intended to be Leader of the 2nd (Tribal) Destroyer Flotilla, but this was not formed as such, and she became instead temporary Leader of the 4th (Home Fleet) Flotilla comprising the 'B' class and Keith (but less Beagle) (Wright & Logan).

Later, when war broke out, Somali *led* Eskimo, Bedouin, Mashona *and* Tartar. *She was involved in the Lofoten Islands raid, and was torpedoed by a U-boat while escorting convoy PQ14.* Ashanti *took her in tow, but she foundered four days later. In this 1942 photo she has a 286 'bedstead' radar aerial and wears the one white band of the 6th (Home Fleet) Flotilla (IWM).*

◀ OPPOSITE

Four 'Tribals' were fitted out as Leaders, but although Sikh *was not among them she later became a Leader in the Mediterranean. This photo shows her so marked in 1942, with Commander G. H. Stokes in command. She was in the* Bismark *action, and, with* Maori, *led the attack on the Italian cruisers. In March 1942, she led the 5th Division (*Lively, Hero *and* Havock) *in the second battle of Sirte, when the splendid quartet ferociously engaged the Italian battleship* Littorio *and three cruisers in the finest traditions of the destroyer. In August, she shared in the 'kill' of U-327, but in September of the same year her luck ran out and she was sunk by shore batteries off Tobruk (IWM).*

Tartar *was another early runner of the class and commissioned as a Divisional Leader.
She thus has a narrow band on each funnel as she leaves Portsmouth in April 1939
(Wright & Logan).*

Flag L and pendants 1 and 8 fly from Zulu's *yardarm as she approaches the Narrows
at the entrance to Portsmouth harbour in September 1938. She had commissioned at
Devonport earlier that month, under Commander J. S. Crawford, RN, for duty in the
Mediterranean. She was in the* Bismark *action and formed the 3rd Division (with*
Hardy) *at the second battle of Sirte.* Zulu *and* Sikh *had an almost 'David and
Jonathan' relationship. After seeing much action together, both ships were sunk off
Tobruk on September 14, 1942. 'And in death they were not divided' (IWM).*

Chapter 5:
The Commonwealth Ships

THESE vessels fall naturally into three groups: the Australian trio; the Tyne-built Canadian units; and the four built in Halifax, Nova Scotia. They were distinguished not just by the geographical position of the shipyard responsible for their construction alone, but also by their distinctive appearance.

The first two Australian ships saw service in the Pacific theatre in World War 2, and the British-built RCN vessels were active in the English Channel and the Bay of Biscay; but the third RAN 'Tribal', and the four built in Canada, were too late for the 1939–45 conflict. Most, however, saw service in the Korean war.

By 1970 all had been scrapped or declared 'for disposal', but to their great credit, the Canadians rescued *Haida* from the clutches of the shipbreakers and she is now part of a Naval Museum in Toronto, Canada.

Like their RN counterparts, the Commonwealth ships were called after indigenous native tribes whose names were mostly unfamiliar to British ears. It was a surprise to many—who had previously lumped all the natives of Australia under the collective title of 'aborigines'—to discover that they had their own tribal names; and similarly, that there were many North American Indians other than the Apache, Comanche, and Shoshone beloved of Holly-wood. (The one well-known name adopted by the RCN was *Souix*, but this

Arunta at speed in 1944 in the SW Pacific war zone. Commissioning in 1942, she soon established herself by sinking the Japanese submarine RO 33, and took part in the battle of Surigao Strait in October 1944. In January 1945, Arunta was the victim of a Kamikaze attack, but was repaired in time to get back in action and joined in the bombardment of Balikpapan in Borneo at the closing stages of the Second World War. She remained active until 1956 (IWM).

The six single Oerlikons and the quad pompom were replaced by Bofors during Arunta's modernization in the early 1950s. Four mountings are concentrated on the after structure—two sided single Bofors, stowed, like the twin 4-inch, muzzle forwards, and a centre-line twin Bofors trained aft. Observe the 'Simple Tachymetric Director' platform at one end of the gundeck and the Squid mortar on the quarterdeck. The '10' on her funnel invoked memories of the Royal Navy's 10th Flotilla in 1945 (Courtesy RAN).

was not a 'Tribal' class ship.) However, before she was completed the name of the last Australian ship—*Kurnai*—was changed to *Bataan* to mark the link forged between General McArthur's American forces and the 'Diggers'. She then became yet another of the 'odd men out' which so frequently turn up in otherwise straightforward name-groups.

AUSTRALIAN 'TRIBALS'

Very properly, Australia opened the innings for the Commonwealth by laying down *Arunta* in November 1939. Understandably, the building pace was a little slow compared with the British shipyards, but there were, of course,

Warramunga saw less service in the Pacific campaign, but was actively employed during the Korean war, when she was D 123. After her modernization in the middle 1950s her appearance closely resembled the refitted Arunta. Like her, Warramunga had a three-figure pendant number (Courtesy RAN).

The Australian 'Tribals' originally had their pendant number prefixed by Flag I superior but this disappeared in 1948 under the general revision. Bataan then changed from I 91 to D 191, because D 91 had already been allocated. Here, in the early 1950s, she prepares to lower boats. She still mounts her quad pompom and depth charge throwers, but has six single Bofors Mk 7 mountings and an unusual—probably American—Warning Radar at her masthead (P. A. Vicary).

inevitable delays in the delivery of specialized equipment from the United Kingdom. *Arunta* was launched a year later and commissioned in March 1942, within weeks of the launch of the second ship *Warramunga*, and the keel-laying of the third, *Kurnai*.

All three vessels came from the shipyard on Cockatoo Island, 'upstream' of Sydney Harbour Bridge and benefited to a greater or lesser extent from war experience and the development of radars and close-range weapons. Each, for instance, had a twin 4-inch in 'X' position from building, a shortened after funnel, and omitted the Vickers machine-guns.

In the first half of the 1950s, when the RN 'Tribals' were only memories, first *Arunta* and then *Warramunga* were taken in hand for refit and modernization. A Squid A/S mortar replaced 'Y' mounting, abaft a lengthened after super-structure; and the close-range armament became six single power 40mm Bofors Mk 7 mounts with a centre-line twin Bofors Mk 5 in place of the quad pompom. These improvements changed *Bataan's* position from being the most modern to becoming the least well equipped, but although she, too, was earmarked for refit, it was ultimately cancelled. She went into reserve in 1956 and did not return to active service.

THE TYNE-BUILT CANADIAN SHIPS

It will be recalled that Vickers were the 'lead' yard for the British ships and this company was awarded the contract for the first four Canadian 'Tribals'. Like the Australian ships, they conformed largely to the developed RN units. Thus, their after funnel was constructed in the 'cut down' manner; a twin 4-inch was fitted on 'X' gundeck; and the depth charge throwers were positioned on the upper deck. At first, they had tripod fore masts, but later exchanged them for lattice structures. *Athabaskan* seems to have been the first to get a new mast—possibly when she was refitted after her early action damage.

The one noticeable difference in the profile of the Canadian ships lay in the area of the after superstructure. The position of the quad pompom was transposed with that of the searchlight and the weapon was mounted on a high platform immediately forward of the 4-inch, where it enjoyed almost un-restricted sky-arcs. No doubt the RN ships would have preferred this arrange-ment too, but the alteration would have entailed considerable work, involving

When the Korean War broke out in 1950, a hurried re-arming of RN and Commonwealth ships was undertaken: and obsolete weapons (which would otherwise have
been retained for the remaining lifetime of the older ships) were replaced by more
modern equipment. Bataan exchanged her old quad pompom for a twin Bofors Mk 5,
whose gunshield can be seen highlighted abaft the second funnel. Here, she shelters
under the lee of a friendly off-shore island, with her fo'c'sle party in 'Arctic clothing'.
This, too, had to be hurriedly issued, for the Korean climate is extreme and, in winter,
the sea frequently freezes over during the night (Courtesy RAN).

Iroquois was the first of the Canadian 'Tribals' and commissioned in early December
1942. This shipbuilder's photograph shows her almost complete, but lacking the
Radar 285 aerial on her R/F director. Her first Commanding Officer was Captain
W. B. L. Holmes (Courtesy Vickers).

OPPOSITE: ▶

In 1945 the surviving three Canadian ships returned home, and are shown here in
column, led by Iroquois. Like her sisters, she saw service in the Channel and Biscay,
where, with the British cruiser Mauritius and the destroyer Ursa, she pounced on
seven German vessels. A sharp engagement resulted in all the enemy ships being sent
to the bottom. Notice that all three ships now have lattice masts (Public Archives of
Canada).

By the late 1940s, Iroquois had been stripped of much of her obsolescent weapon equipment and became the Headquarters of the Senior Officer, Reserve Ships. In August 1949, when this photo was taken, she lay at anchor at Baddeck, Nova Scotia, still wearing her old pendant number (Public Archives of Canada).

the repositioning of all the equipment on the emergency steering platform.

Vickers were able to take advantage of the improved close-range weapon situation and worked in six Oerlikon mountings—one pair on redesigned bridge sponsons, a second pair between the funnels and a third abreast the searchlight. The after pair adopted the space vacated by the depth charge throwers (which had been dropped one deck).

The first ship in commission was *Iroquois*, who beat *Athabaskan* by a few weeks, having exchanged designated names with her on the stocks. She emerged with single 20mm mountings and few radars, and it would appear likely that *Athabaskan* was similar when built. Photographs of the ill-starred second runner are rare, for she was very short-lived. Those that do exist, show her with a lattice fore mast and six *twin* Oerlikons—all probably the outcome of her first repairs: a probability that gains credence when one examines the second Tyne-built pair.

These were *Huron* and *Haida*, who both had tripod masts—an unlikely reversion, had the earlier *Athabaskan* been given a lattice in the first instance. They also showed other changes. Each had six twin Oerlikons and a radar Type 271 'lantern' in place of the searchlight. Further, by this time, the Destroyer DCT had become obsolescent, and was omitted from the bridge. Instead, the entire fire control of the main armament centred on a variant of the R/F Director, known as the Mk III (W). It was almost identical with the earlier Mk II (W) but accommodated an extra crew member—the Rate Officer—whose duty was to assess the course and speed of a surface target.

In 1951, Iroquois *emerged from a long modernization refit that radically altered her. Twin 4-inch replaced her forward 4·7s and a US 3-inch/50 calibre twin was mounted aft in place of the original 4-inch. She retained her old DCT on the bridge, but the R/F director was removed in favour of the US Mk 63 Director, controlling her forward weapons. The system radar aerial can just be seen on 'B' gunshield. Notice the heavy lattice foremast and the US radar scanner on its head, but that she still has British Radar 293 on the topmast, and 291 aft on the short mainmast (Public Archives of Canada).*

In September 1957 Iroquois *visited Portsmouth, by which time funnel cowls had been fitted and whip aerials for her improved communications. Note the long after superstructure and the port Squid mortar on the quarterdeck. She was unmanned after 1964 (Wright & Logan).*

The ill-fated Athabaskan *(I), fully fitted out. In August 1943 she became a victim of one of Germany's 'secret weapons'—a remotely controlled glider-bomb—but was repaired in time to join in the Channel and Biscay sweeps of 1944. In April of that year she was torpedoed by the German torpedo-boat T27 and blew-up with heavy loss of life (IWM).*

THE HALIFAX 'TRIBALS'

The original intention of the two Dominions had been to equip themselves with a flotilla of 'Tribals' each, as counterparts to the first RN order. In the event, Australia cancelled all save three but Canada persisted with her ideas to the extent that when she lost *Athabaskan* in 1944 she added an extra ship to her own building plans as a replacement.

The first two ships, *Micmac* and *Nootka*—launched in 1943 and 1944 respectively—conformed pretty well to the second Tyne-built pair, except that they were given a lattice mast while on the stocks. Their three twin 4·7s were the last to be fitted for service under the White Ensign and were specially modified to take the improved fuze-setting machines by then in plentiful supply. *Micmac* shipped a quad pompom in the 'Canadian' position, but *Nootka* was better armed with 'sided' twin Bofors on the same site.

In the final pair, the armament was completely revised to take advantage of late- and post-war developments. The ships could not accommodate the twin 4·5-inch Mk IV mounting of the RN 'Battle' class, so both ships were given the best alternative—the RPC version of the twin 4-inch—and had four such weapons in the conventional positions. The (then) latest RN Destroyer Fire Control system, employing a Mk 6 director, was adopted and the close-range armament tidied-up to 40mm calibre.

◀ OPPOSITE

Athabaskan was the second of the Canadian 'Tribals', entering the water in November 1941 (having exchanged names with Iroquois on the stocks), and Commander G. R. Miles, O.B.E., was appointed in command in December 1942. In this shot she is not yet fully fitted out and lacks her Mk II (W) and her radars. Twin Oerlikon Mk 5 mountings are fitted in pairs on the bridge-wings, between the funnels and above the after Carley float skids; close to the latter are her single depth charge throwers. Observe how the close-range sky arcs were improved by the transposition of the pompom and the searchlight platform. This undated photograph was possibly taken after her first action damage had been repaired, for she has a lattice mainmast (Public Archives of Canada).

The twin Bofors Mk 5 was the successor to the quad pompom, but like the single Mk 7, was produced too late for any British 'Tribals'. It could be aimed by a layer and trainer using hand-cranks; by the layer alone, in local power; or in the primary mode in RPC from the adjacent director sight. To allow longer sustained firing the twin barrels were fitted with water-cooling jackets, giving them a stocky profile. The portable girders clipped to the substantial gunshield were erected over the open top of the mounting to support a gun cover. Notice the layer's access door clipped shut; the black armament broadcast loudspeaker above his position, and the canvas wind-dodger, laced to the director platform guardrails (Anthony Peters).

The sky above Plymouth was dotted with barrage balloons in May 1944 when this photograph of Huron was taken. She had been accepted from Vickers in July of the previous year, and was one of the pair to be given a Radar 271 'lantern'. The old 'Destroyer DCT' was already obsolescent and was omitted. Instead, she had a variant of the R/F director family, known as the Mk III (W) to control her main armament in either surface or anti-aircraft fire. Within weeks of this photo being taken, she was in action against German surface vessels off Cherbourg (Public Archives of Canada).

OPPOSITE: ▶

Huron was taken in hand for interim modernization in 1946, when she landed her old twin 4·7s. The forward mountings were replaced by twin 4-inch and 'Y' by a Squid mortar, but she retained her pompom, Mk III (W) director, and light lattice mast. Four single Bofors were fitted in what were to become the standard positions of the class (Public Archives of Canada).

MODERNISATION

The first major post-war alteration came with the supercession of the 4·7s by RPC twin 4-inch in the Tyne-built ships and in the first Canadian pair. Similarly, single 40mm Bofors replaced their Oerlikons and twin Mk 5s began to occupy the position held for so many years by the quad pompom. By 1951, 'Y' gun had been landed to make room for Squid A/S mortars; and about this time all seven ships had an American twin 3-inch/50 calibre mounting on 'X' gun deck. Controlled by the US Mk 63 Gunfire Control System, it was an independent self-controlled unit, incorporating its own radar. The 'dish-shaped' aerial was mounted on the elevating gun cradle and full 'blind fire' tracking against unseen targets could be carried out.

The system was adopted by the Royal Navy for the (then) recently modernized carrier *Victorious*, so that she might be armed with up-to-date 3-inch AA guns with a high rate of fire. At this time, there were several elderly 6-inch gun cruisers still running in the Royal Navy and to bring their 4-inch AA armament to similar fire control standards a modified US system was produced to suit these guns. It was not feasible to mount the aerial on the 4-inch elevating structure itself, so a special variant of the radar was designed for fitting on the British 4-inch gunshield.

The Canadians took advantage of this scheme and made sweeping changes to their 'Tribals'. From contemporary photographs, it seems that *Micmac* was the testbed, because in 1952 she had a 3-inch twin in 'B' position, but no 'A' gun—a set-up reminiscent of other trial installations. In due course the five ships with a R/F director had it removed and adopted the United States system for a main armament that now comprised only 'A' and 'B' mountings. A minor variant resulted, for the only ship with the old-fashioned DCT—*Iroquois*—retained it for surface fire control, but exchanged her R/F Director Mk II (W) for the US Mk 63 sight. Almost the opposite obtained in the other four. They mounted the American sight on the unoccupied DCT position but kept a stripped down version of the Mk III (W) as a simple surface director.

These fire control changes apart, the seven Canadian ships became almost identical. Heavy lattice masts carried an impressive array of radars; twin Squid mortars occupied the quarter-deck; and all had two twin 4-inch, a twin 3-inch,

Portsmouth welcomed Huron *in May 1966, not long before she went into Reserve. By this time she had again been modernized, receiving the twin 3-inch aft, and the heavy lattice mast. The Mk III (W) was stripped down to function as a simple surface control sight and 4-inch AA fire was conducted from the Mk 63 director mounted on a pedestal in the centre of the bridge (Wright & Logan).*

four single Bofors, and a quad torpedo tube mounting. The single Bofors of the first five were fitted directly on to power twin Oerlikon mountings, but *Cayuga* and *Athabaskan* had the improved single Bofors Mk 7 proper.

Later in the 1950s, cowls were added to the funnels of these splendid ships, which gave them a faintly 'Germanic' look, but in no way detracted from their already rakish appearance. With a high, white bow-wave, with the sun shining on their light grey upperworks, and the red splash of the Maple Leaf emblem on the after funnel, they carried the tradition of the 'Tribals' well into the 1960s. It is comforting, indeed, to know that one is preserved for posterity in Toronto.

A grand total of 27 'Tribals' was launched between June 1937 and May 1946 and their eight-gun broadside has never been equalled by any other class of British destroyer. How proud their ship's companies must have been of them; and what famous names emerged from among their commanding officers.

The years have slipped by and the Fleet has diminished. The ships and even the calibre of the guns has changed: but, happily, the calibre of the men has not. So although, perhaps, the current class of 'Tribals' of the 1970s have less presence than those of 30 years ago, they would, no doubt, give as good account of themselves in war as did their illustrious forebears.

Unless one could distinguish the figure 5 from 6 with the naked eye, it was almost impossible to differentiate Haida *(shown here off Portsmouth in May 1955) from* Huron *(opposite). Like her,* Haida *had a full modernization in the early 1950s. She went into Reserve in 1965. Compare with original appearance shown at bottom of opposite page. (Wright & Logan).*

Although the Halifax shipyard launched their first 'Tribal' in 1943, she was not commissioned until September 1945, when hostilities had ceased. This ship was Micmac, *seen here carrying out trials in July of that year. She looked very like the Tyne-built ships and mounted the usual three twin 4·7s, a twin 4-inch and a quad pompom. Again, the DCT was omitted and she was built with a lattice mast (Public Archives of Canada).*

◀ OPPOSITE

Haida *was the last of the Tyne-built ships and like her sisters ran from Plymouth, which she is shown leaving in July 1944. Notice the prominent Mk III (W) director, the HF/DF aerial on the pole mast aft, and the 271 'lantern'. The latter has an IFF aerial projecting above it, and long-range air warning is taken care of by the 291 on the fore topmast (Public Archives of Canada).*

By June 1954, when she visited Portsmouth, Micmac conformed to the modernized profile but later had funnel cowls added. It is interesting to note that the re-build omitted close-range weapons from the bridge wings (Wright & Logan).

Nootka was the next Canadian 'Tribal', entering service in 1946. She was the last to fit twin 4·7-inch in the three accepted positions and had an unusual close-range weapon layout. Twin Oerlikons were mounted on the bridge-wings and between the funnels, supplementing a sided pair of twin Bofors Mk 5, which are clearly shown in this photograph, taken in September 1948 as she refuelled from the Canadian carrier Magnificent. The twin 4·7-inch gunshields have been widened to accommodate the modern AA shell fuze-setting machines and the main armament is controlled by a D/P Mk III (W) director. Notice the depth charge throwers abreast the high Bofors gundeck and the centre-line 'trap' over the stern (Public Archives of Canada).

Nootka *gives a fine impression of speed during her full-power trials off Dartmouth, Nova Scotia, in September 1950. She now has a 4-inch calibre main armament; has omitted close-range weapons from the bridge; and has received single Bofors between the funnels (Public Archives of Canada).*

Like most Commonwealth 'Tribals', Nootka *saw action in the Korean war. Here, she bombards Songjin in May 1951, in support of United Nations land forces (Public Archives of Canada).*

With 'all mod. cons.' and funnel cowls, Nootka *arrives off Portsmouth in September 1957. In 1946 her Captain was Commander H. S. Rayner, D.S.C., who had previously commanded* Huron *; and in 1950 it was Commander A. B. F. Fraser, D.S.C. and Bar, CD (Commander, Canadian Destroyers, Far East) (Wright & Logan).*

Cayuga *was the third of the Halifax-built ships and differed from the earlier 'Tribals' in being built with a main armament of four twin 4-inch, controlled by a Mk 6 Director. This photograph was taken in September 1950, while she was bombarding the coast of Korea. Notice the two steam-driven cable-holders and the seizing between the cables. Her Commanding Officer, Captain J. V. Brock, D.S.C., was at one time Commander, Canadian Destroyers, Pacific (Public Archives of Canada).*

Cayuga's *modernization followed the usual pattern, except that she retained her Mk 6 director. She was off Pangyang Do, Korea, when this picture was taken in September 1954, but by that time the Korean war had ended (Public Archives of Canada).*

When Cayuga *visited Portsmouth in October 1962 the only marked change in her appearance was the addition of a streamlined fibreglass shield to the 3-inch twin aft. This automatic gun mounting had a complicated ammunition feed system, which was vulnerable to prolonged bad weather (Wright & Logan).*

The second Athabaskan *was the last of the 'Tribal' class, and was completed in 1948. The January snow of Halifax, Nova Scotia, lay thick in the woods as she proceeded to sea on trials. Observe her four twin 4-inch mountings, the big Mk 6 director and the high-set pair of twin Bofors Mk 5 aft. The cupola on her modern torpedo tube mounting should also be noted (Public Archives of Canada).*

Appendix 1: The Ship's Badges

THE 16 RN 'Tribals' had the standard shield-shaped crests, but this pattern was abandoned after the war and most ships now have a round badge, irrespective of their type. The post-war 'Tribal' class GP frigates have this round badge, but adopted the design of their earlier namesakes.

The designs themselves were fairly straightforward, showing a typical tribal head or an indigenous animal, but *Bedouin*, *Gurkha* and *Zulu* used appropriate weapons. *Sikh* had two traditional emblems—the parasol and the lion; *Maori* had a good-luck charm called a 'Tiki' and the motto 'Aki aki, Kia Kaha'—'Push on, be brave'; and *Mashona* used a representation of the bird carved in soapstone discovered at Great Zimbabwe with the motto 'Chisarayi'—'Stay in peace'.

TRIBAL NAMES AND AREAS

Afridi	NW Frontier, India
Ashanti	Ghana
Bedouin	Nomadic Arab
Cossack	SE Russia
Eskimo	Northern North America and Greenland
Gurkha	Nepal
Maori	New Zealand
Mashona	Southern Rhodesia
Matabele	Southern Rhodesia
Mohawk	Canada
Nubian	Between Sudan and Egypt
Punjabi	NW India
Sikh	The Punjab
Somali	The 'Horn of Africa'
Tartar	Central Asia
Zulu	Natal, South Africa
Arunta, *Kurnai*, *Warramunga*	Australian aboriginies
Canadian ships	Canadian Indian tribes

The final development of the 'Tribals' typified by HMCS Athabaskan. *The fibreglass shield on the twin 3-inch became an extra recognition feature of the final pair, although they were in any case immediately identified by their director. Commander A. E. Fox was in command when Athabaskan visited Portsmouth in October 1962, in company with her nearest sister ship. In 1959 her Captain rejoiced in the title CANCOMCORTRONTHREE (Canadian Commander, Third Escort Squadron) (Wright & Logan).*

Appendix 2:
Fire Control Transmissions

THE diagrammatic drawing opposite gives a complete picture of the main fire control system of the original 'Tribal' class ships. Follow the key numbers on the drawing in the text below. The main external elements of the system, ie, guns, directors, and radar aerials are, of course, visible in the pictures in this book. The AFCC and FKC were located in the Transmitting Station (TS) sited below the bridge at main deck level, from where data was fed to the gun mounts.

(1) A rotatable graticule in the Control Officer's binocular sight, aligned to the target fuselage, gave angle of presentation.

(2) The DCT training transmission ensured that the R/F Director ranged on the correct target in surface fire.

(3) High angle/low angle multi-pole changeover switch in the Transmitting Station.

(4) Inclination, by definition, is the angle between the line of sight produced and the target course, measured 'left' or 'right'.

(5) In HA fire, the 'cross-roll' motor in the AFCC was used to combine director training with total HA training corrections and the gun training motor in the surface fire control calculator was common to both modes of operation.

(6) A matching receiver compared the calculated range with that derived from radar and/or rangefinder.

(7) If calculated range did not accurately match radar range, it indicated that the change of range generated by the AFCC was in error—usually because target speed and/or inclination had been wrongly assessed.

(8) A constant speed electric motor drove an integrator, which itself produced the change of range referred to in (7) above.

(9) Corrections could also be made to the calculator by adjusting its solution on the evidence of the fall of shot. If, for example, the shells persistently fell short, the Control Officer might order 'Up 100 yards', which was set as a 'spotting correction'.

(10) The R/F Director sight was not stabilized and its movements in elevation to track a target included those necessary to counteract ship's motion. The roll unit subtracted these oscillations to produce the steady angle of sight upon which predictions depended.

(11) The FKC constant speed motor drove a device which controlled the setting of the time fuzes on HA shell, and also gave the exact moment to fire.

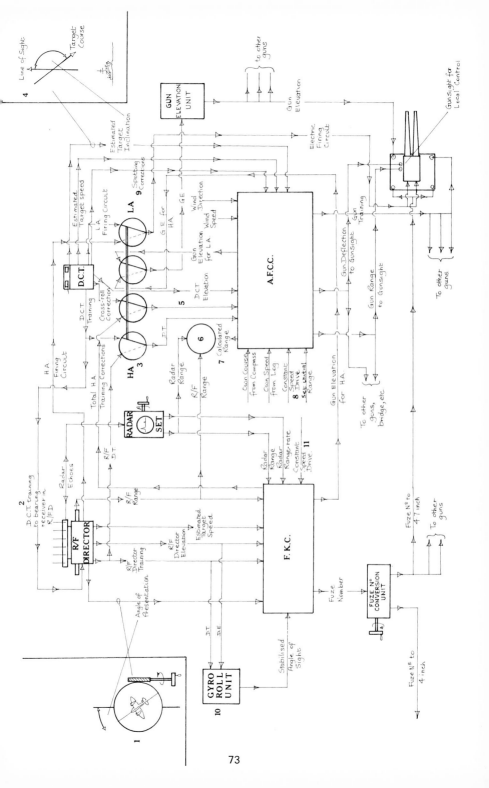

73

Appendix 3:
General Arrangement
Drawings

(1) Pre-war ('as first fitted')

4 × twin 4·7-inch
1 × quad pompom
2 × quad Vickers machine-gun

1 : 600 scale

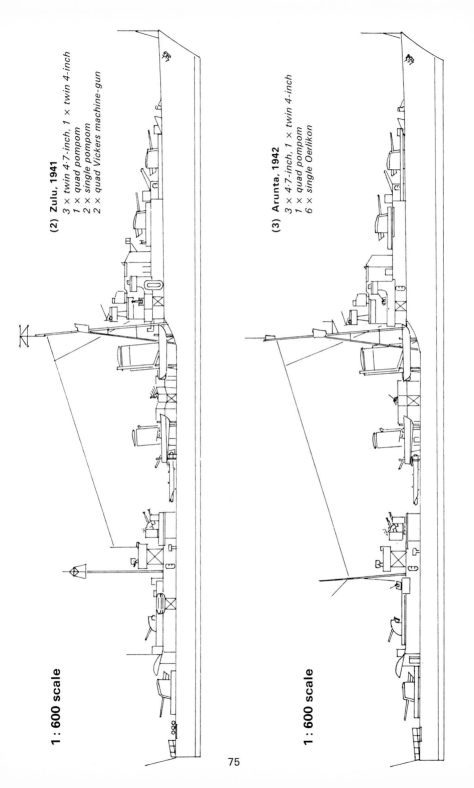

1 : 600 scale

(2) Zulu, 1941
3 × twin 4·7-inch, 1 × twin 4-inch
1 × quad pompom
2 × single pompom
2 × quad Vickers machine-gun

1 : 600 scale

(3) Arunta, 1942
3 × 4·7-inch, 1 × twin 4-inch
1 × quad pompom
6 × single Oerlikon

75

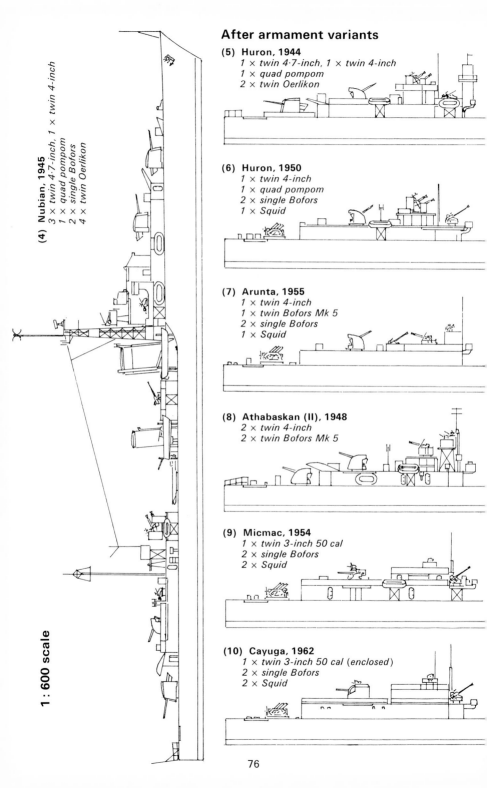

1 : 600 scale

(4) Nubian, 1945
3 × twin 4·7-inch, 1 × twin 4-inch
1 × quad pompom
2 × single Bofors
4 × twin Oerlikon

After armament variants

(5) Huron, 1944
1 × twin 4·7-inch, 1 × twin 4-inch
1 × quad pompom
2 × twin Oerlikon

(6) Huron, 1950
1 × twin 4-inch
1 × quad pompom
2 × single Bofors
1 × Squid

(7) Arunta, 1955
1 × twin 4-inch
1 × twin Bofors Mk 5
2 × single Bofors
1 × Squid

(8) Athabaskan (II), 1948
2 × twin 4-inch
2 × twin Bofors Mk 5

(9) Micmac, 1954
1 × twin 3-inch 50 cal
2 × single Bofors
2 × Squid

(10) Cayuga, 1962
1 × twin 3-inch 50 cal (enclosed)
2 × single Bofors
2 × Squid

Forward armament variants

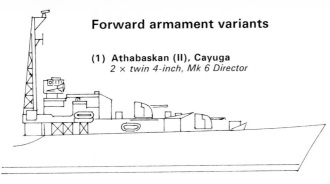

(1) Athabaskan (II), Cayuga
2 × twin 4-inch, Mk 6 Director

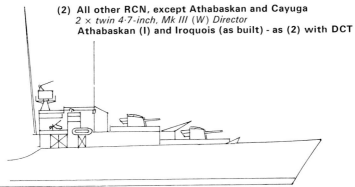

(2) All other RCN, except Athabaskan and Cayuga
2 × twin 4·7-inch, Mk III (W) Director
Athabaskan (I) and Iroquois (as built) - as (2) with DCT

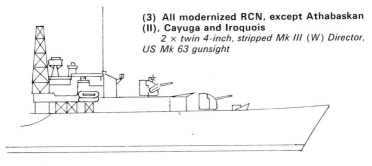

(3) All modernized RCN, except Athabaskan (II), Cayuga and Iroquois
2 × twin 4-inch, stripped Mk III (W) Director, US Mk 63 gunsight

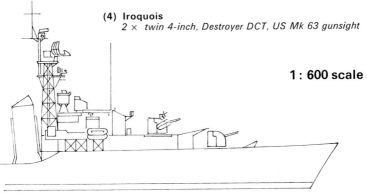

(4) Iroquois
2 × twin 4-inch, Destroyer DCT, US Mk 63 gunsight

1 : 600 scale

Appendix 4: Chronological List and Details

NAME	PENDANT NUMBERS			COM-PLETED	BUILDER	DISPOSAL AND REMARKS
	FLAG SUPERIOR	FIRST	FINAL			
AFRIDI		07		MAY '38	VICKERS ARMSTRONG	Bombed and sunk off Namsos, Norway, May '40
COSSACK		03		JUNE '38	VICKERS ARMSTRONG	Foundered off Gibraltar after torpedoed, North Atlantic, Oct. '41
MOHAWK		31		SEPT. '38	THORNYCROFT	Torpedoed by Italian destroyer off Cape Bon : sunk by *Jervis*, Apr.' 41
ZULU		18		SEPT. '38	STEPHEN	Foundered off Tobruk after bombed, Sept. '42
SIKH		82		OCT. '38	STEPHEN	Sunk by shore batteries off Tobruk, Sept. '42
GURKHA		20		OCT. '38	FAIRFIELD	Bombed and sunk off Stavanger, Norway, April '40
NUBIAN	L UNTIL 1939 · F UNTIL 1940 · G FROM 1940	36	NOT CHANGED	DEC. '38	THORNYCROFT	Scrapped, June '49
SOMALI		33		DEC. '38	SWAN HUNTER	Foundered in tow after torpedoed off Ireland, Sept. '42
ASHANTI		51		DEC. '38	DENNY	Scrapped, March '49
ESKIMO		75		DEC. '38	VICKERS ARMSTRONG	Scrapped, June '49
MAORI		24		JAN. '39	FAIRFIELD	Bombed in Malta. Feb. '42 : raised and scuttled, July '45
MATABELE		26		JAN. '39	SCOTTS	Torpedoed in Barents Sea, Jan. '42
TARTAR		43		MAR. '39	SWAN HUNTER	Scrapped, Dec. '48
BEDOUIN		67		MAR. '39	DENNY	Torpedoed in tow after shell damage, June '42
MASHONA		59		MAR. '39	VICKERS ARMSTRONG	Bombed and sunk off Ireland. May '41
PUNJABI		21		MAR. '39	SCOTTS	Rammed and sunk by HMS *King George V*, May '42

NAME	PENDANT NUMBERS			COMPLETED	BUILDER	DISPOSAL AND REMARKS
	FLAG SUPERIOR	FIRST	FINAL			
ARUNTA	I UNTIL '48 / D FROM '48	30	130	MAR. '42	COCKATOO	Scrapped '68
WARRAMUNGA		41	123	? '43		Scrapped '68
BATAAN		91	191	MAY '45		Scrapped '62
IROQUOIS		89	217	DEC. '42	VICKERS ARMSTRONG	Scrapped '66
ATHABASKAN (I)		07		FEB. '43		Torpedoed off North-West France, April '44
HURON	G UNTIL 1950 / NONE AFTER '50	24	216	JULY '43		Scrapped '65
HAIDA		63	215	SEPT. '43		Naval Museum, Toronto, Canada, '64
MICMAC		10	214	SEPT. '45	HALIFAX SHIPYARD	Scrapped '64
NOOTKA		96	213	OCT. '46		Scrapped '64
CAYUGA		04	218	OCT. '47		Scrapped '64
ATHABASKAN (II)	R UNTIL 1950 / NONE AFTER '50	79	219	JAN. '48		For disposal ('70)

BASIC DETAILS

Length: 355½ft (between perpendiculars)
377ft (overall)
Beam: 36½ft
Depth: 21½ft
Full Load Draft: Approx 13½ft
Displacement: Approx 2,500 tons, full load
Machinery: Parsons Single Reduction Geared Turbines
2 Shafts = 44,000 S.H.P.
Three Admiralty 3-Drum Boilers
300 p.si. at 620°F
Oil Fuel approx 500 tons
Complement (Peace): 190 (Leaders 219)

Appendix 5:
'Tribal' Commanding Officers reaching Flag Rank in the Royal Navy

NAME	SHIP/DATE	DECORATIONS/ FLAG RANK/DATE
Cdr. Buzzard	*Gurkha* 1940	C.B., D.S.O., O.B.E. Rear Admiral 1951
Cdr. Eaton	*Mohawk* 1939	C.B., D.S.O. Vice Admiral 1954
Lt. Cdr./Cdr. Holland-Martin	*Tartar* 1938 *Nubian* 1942	D.S.O., D.S.C. and Bar Rear Admiral 1955
Capt. McLaughlin	*Mashona* 1939	C.B., D.S.O. Rear Admiral 1949
Cdr. Micklethwaite	*Eskimo* 1938	C.B., D.S.O. and 2 Bars Rear Admiral 1950
Lt. Morgan	*Eskimo* 1942	C.B., D.S.C. Rear Admiral 1965
Capt. Nicholson	*Somali* 1938	C.B., D.S.O., D.S.C. Vice Admiral 1948
Cdr. Onslow	*Ashanti* 1941	C.B., D.S.O. and 3 Bars Vice Admiral 1955
Cdr. Selby	*Mashona* 1940	C.B., D.S.O., D.S.C. Vice Admiral 1948
Cdr. Sherbrooke	*Cossack* 1939 *Matabele* 1940	V.C., C.B., D.S.O. Rear Admiral 1951
Cdr. Stokes	*Sikh* 1940	C.B., D.S.C. Rear Admiral 1952
Cdr. Tyrwhitt	*Tartar* 1942	D.S.O., D.S.C. and Bar Rear Admiral 1955
Capt. Vian	*Afridi* 1940 *Cossack* 1940	G.C.B., K.B.E., D.S.O. and 2 Bars, LL.D. Admiral of the Fleet